The Life Science Executive's
FUNDRAISING MANIFESTO

BEST PRACTICES FOR IDENTIFYING CAPITAL
IN THE BIOTECH AND MEDTECH ARENAS

Dennis Ford

LIFE SCIENCE
NATION
Connecting Products, Services & Capital

PUBLISHED BY
Life Science Nation
9-B Hamilton Place, Boston, MA 02108
www.lifesciencenation.com

Printed in the United States of America.
ISBN: 978-0-9903251-0-9
First Edition: 10 9 8 7 6 5 4 3 2 1

For information about special discounts or bulk purchases, please contact Life Science Nation: 617-600-0668 or sales@lifesciencenation.com.

Cover Design: Red Door Media (www.reddoormedia.com) and Nono Hu,
    Marketing Manager, Life Science Nation
Interior Design and Composition: Marian Hartsough (mjhart53@gmail.com)
Editor: Wendy Herlich (wendywendyh@gmail.com)
Cartoonist: Ryan Hannus (hannusjobbus@gmail.com)
Project Management: Neuhaus Publishing (www.neuhauspublishing.com)

Contents

Introduction

Dennis Ford

If you have picked up this book, you are probably a life science entrepreneur who has reached the exciting phase of development when you are actively seeking investors in your firm and product. Congratulations! Growing a company to this stage is not an easy process, and although attracting funding isn't either, if you take the right approach, winning an allocation can become not only an achievable milestone but also a feat you accomplish repeatedly.

I founded my company Life Science Nation (LSN) to bring sales and marketing awareness to the life science community. LSN's goal is to help educate scientists in the rudimentary skills needed to brand, message, and market their companies from a fundraising perspective. We aim to achieve this in two ways: first, by teaching the basic skills needed to aggregate a list of potential global investors that are a fit for the scientists' products and services. Secondly, we instruct how to efficiently and effectively reach out to these potential investors, start a dialogue that fosters a relationship, and ultimately secure capital allocations.

Before I began this work, I was the CEO of a company similar to LSN, where I helped pioneer a system for uncovering global institutional investors and gauging their appetite regarding investing in hedge funds, private equity funds, and venture capital (VC) funds. The methodology used to capture and curate this valuable data was developed in part by a research team that would cold call and canvass these investors. The team would conduct a 21-point survey in the form of a one-on-one interview with each investor that elucidated any current investment mandates they had. In short, we figured out where the cash was and specifically who had the mandate to deploy it!

Finding out which investors had capital and where they wanted to invest it was a markedly different strategy from the status quo of fundraising tactics. At the time, the marketing paradigm in the alternative investment industry was a shotgun approach; managers blindly reached out to any potential investor, regardless of fit, and promoted their funds. This method was highly inefficient and ineffective for both fund managers and investors.

We helped changed this paradigm by introducing a marketing process that was investor focused: fundraising executives would contact investors who had declared an interest in their type of fund during interviews with trained research staff. Gathering this level of interest, as declared directly by an investor to a researcher, is the gold standard for data profiling. We understood that fund marketers could improve their success rate if they marketed to active investors with a current interest in their type of solution.

After working with fundraisers in the alternative finance space for six years, I wanted to bring my expertise into the area of the life sciences and channel my fundraising experience toward the goal of helping to moving science forward. I had witnessed firsthand the trend of institutional investors (endowments, foundations, and even some pensions) and family offices demonstrating an interest in direct life science investment. This trend was partly due to a desire to have more direct control of investments and save money on management fees. It was also driven by an increased philanthropic interest in medical research, as family offices and institutions began putting their resources toward the fight to eradicate certain diseases and illnesses that impact their families and people around the world. This migration of capital created a direct investment trend that continues to gain momentum to this day.

Where to go to find who has capital and is a fit for your firm is the conundrum in the life science arena. Too often life science marketers focus regionally instead of taking advantage of the global market. LSN enables the creation of global target lists (GTLs) for both the sellers and the buyers in the life science arena; this helps both parties qualify and filter each other, thus facilitating meaningful dialogue from the outset.

LSN does this with the help of our one-of-a-kind life science investor database, which covers 10 categories of investors, and an emerging biotech and medtech company database, which profiles the hard-to-find emerging players with the latest technological advancements. As LSN has grown, we have expanded our global reach, profiling investors and companies in the Americas, Europe, the Middle East, and Asia; we now have investor coverage in close to 100 countries. In short, LSN is a global matchmaking platform for the life science industry.

I have been called a street-savvy tech entrepreneur because of my direct outbound selling style, which proselytizes using data profiling to find targets that are a fit for your product, and getting out of the office and in front of potential investors to compete hard for the capital. I have also been labeled as a maverick contrarian due to my belief that this is the ideal way to learn and be successful. Too many executives listen to the so-called marketing experts who give them the impression that large social networks and a website will function like a beacon and bring business to them. Others want to believe in solutions that are too good to be true, for example, that crowdsourcing and funding portals will magically solve their capital problems.

However, I stick to my guns and my proven, rudimentary selling methodology; the only way to find capital is to go out into the market and create dialogue with investors, which can develop into relationships that eventually foster the allocation of funds. This starts with picking up the phone, arranging a meeting, and selling yourself, your team, and your product. It is a long, arduous process; you will never attend only a few meetings and then get a check.

When I first launched LSN in 2012 and entered the life science fundraising arena, I was introduced to a CEO who was trying to raise six million dollars to get a small molecule into a phase IIa clinical study. After a few meetings, I asked if I could take a look at his marketing collateral to see how he was going about branding, messaging, and positioning his firm. When he finally sent the material over, I could see why he was having trouble.

There was no tagline, elevator pitch, or executive summary to be found. There was a PowerPoint presentation, which consisted of 90 cumbersome and incomprehensible pages. Most of the words in the document were between 15 and 25 characters long and were terms I was completely unfamiliar with. The firm had developed a small molecule with a primary application of eradicating malignant cancerous tumors, but their marketing materials indicated that the molecule could also help with Alzheimer's and many other indications. I could not figure out whether they had a platform for developing products or one single product that had many applications.

There were other problems, too. There was no logo that clearly defined the company; the home page of their custom-designed website inexplicably featured an image of a pastoral, wooded setting. When I actually met the team, which consisted of reputable, seasoned scientists who were world renowned, I discovered that they had known each other for so long that when they discussed things and answered my questions, I always felt as though I was in the middle of a family dispute.

I wasted no time in telling them that if they wanted to successfully market themselves to life science investors, they were going to have to make some radical adjustments. Over the course of eight grueling weeks, we developed a compelling brand for their firm and came up with marketing materials that were concise and easy to understand. We created a tagline that described in only a few words what they had invented, an elevator pitch that clearly stated their value and their distinctive technology in only a few sentences, and a cogent two-page executive summary. We concentrated on only one indication: oncology.

We gave the website an overhaul, crafting it so that the 90-page slide deck could be easily navigated, and ensured that their innovative small molecule was showcased with plenty of trial data to back up and validate the technology story. We also counseled them on how to make their personal presentation reflect the strength of their company and product and encouraged them to get on the same page so they could begin to work together as a team. Fifteen months later I received a phone call from the CEO; he reported that the firm had secured the six million dollars they needed from a European family office to get to the next trial phase and that he was so pleased and grateful for the help he had received from LSN.

On another occasion, I spoke with a scientist who liked the fact that my firm tracked non-VC investors but ultimately was too comfortable with his existing VC and angel network to look elsewhere, believing he would be diverting his efforts. One year later he called me back in desperation; he had made no progress with his network and was running out of time. My team assisted him in compiling a list of investors to go after and setting up a cloud-based application infrastructure to organize this list; they also helped with the associated tasks of conducting an outbound fundraising campaign. Within the first month of using the product, he stated that he had tripled the number of discussions he was having with non-VC and angel investors and that he had come to understand that he needed to be working constantly to uncover new ones. He reported that he had met several investors that were a great fit, and felt that a few of them might lead to allocations.

I met another CEO at a speaking engagement who, during the question-and-answer phase, gingerly raised his hand and said, "Let me be very clear on this, Mr. Ford. Are you suggesting that it is acceptable for me to call someone I don't know and ask them to invest in my product?" I replied that yes, this was called "canvassing," and that it is a technique that has been used in sales and marketing for decades.

After the meeting one of my sales executives gave him a demonstration of the LSN investor database and told him how we could help. He had a great product in a hot industry sector and had done fairly well in developing his branding and messaging, so we started to work with him on how to canvass and reach out via phone calls and emails. After a few weeks, we had a status meeting, and he said he was just not getting a response.

We came to realize that although he was a brilliant scientist who was running a sound firm, his outreach and follow-up were halfhearted. He was stumbling when it came to presenting himself, and moreover, he didn't have the resources or the capability to devote the time to the tedious, mundane job of following up and scheduling the introductory calls and meetings. At our urging, he hired a business development employee whose personality was a better fit for the job and whose sole focus was to canvass and set up meetings. This led to the development of relationships with several investors, and last I heard, that CEO is getting close to closing his financing round.

There are many more such tales from the life science fundraising road that I could share with you. Indeed, in the two years since LSN has launched, we have helped over 100 clients learn about the art and science of executing outbound campaigns. This book was written in order to share those valuable insights and tips with a wider audience and to shed light on what a successful life science fundraising executive needs to understand before heading into the market to get discussions going with investors.

You will soon see that the fields of experimental science and marketing share many characteristics. Both favor an approach that is essentially a numbers game, involving tasks that are tedious, mundane, and repetitive. Both require immense focus and perseverance. Though a person may endure hundreds of rejections or failures, just one positive result can change everything. The similarity between these two worlds that otherwise seem so different can work in your favor. Though you may be uncomfortable with the idea of marketing and fundraising, or feel you are in over your head when it comes to selling yourself and your product, odds are that you are more capable than you realize. Good luck and good selling!

The Legal Landscape and Requirements for Fundraising

As you may already know, for a multitude of reasons, attorneys are vital when you commit to launching a start-up. The issues they help with range from figuring out how to distribute equity to employees, investors, and partners to making the end-of-the-road choices leading up to your exit. You must always remember that as your company evolves, its legal needs will change from stage to stage. That is why you need to take the time to familiarize yourself with the myriad of legal issues that will surely surface as you move your firm along the path in its development, from early stage to mid-stage to late stage.

Your first epiphany might be that the lawyer who sets up your company structure may not be the same lawyer who protects your intellectual property (IP). The lawyer who helps craft pre- and post-investment documents isn't necessarily going to be the one who sits at the table and hammers out a distribution deal. The law firm you use to conduct an initial public offering (IPO) may not be the same firm that does a merger and acquisitions (M&A) deal. Suffice it to say, if you did have a law firm that could cover all the permutations of a life science entity, it would be costing you a pretty penny!

A recurring question for a start-up entrepreneur is the old adage: How do you eat an elephant? And the best answer is . . . one bite at a time. The legal elephant can be consumed the same way. The typical order of operations begins with determining how to protect your IP, setting up the proper structure for a business entity, and understanding how equity and dilution will impact the company as it grows and morphs from stage to stage. In the early stage, you want to make sure that you don't give away the farm and that you plan for later growth and development. It is easy to make a mistake out of context that can come back and bite you at a later stage, so forethought and sound legal counsel are required. The good news is that you are not the first life science start-up, so there is a wealth of data and information that can serve as an effective guide to the challenges you will be facing.

New funding mechanisms and rules and regulations introduced by the Jumpstart Our Business Startups (JOBS) Act have created new possibilities for companies seeking to raise capital. Crowdfunding brings with it distinct limitations on how much can be raised in a year but might be a good fit for early stage companies that need some seed money in order to get off the ground. The loosening of Regulation D, which governs how an entrepreneur can solicit and pursue "Accredited Investors," has also changed the game for many life science entrepreneurs. In addition, the JOBS Act has, for the first time, allowed companies to "test the waters" by confidentially initiating the registration process before launching a formal IPO. Each of these developments has major implications for how companies will be able to get the funding they need in order to move into the next stage of development.

It would take several books to explain all the legal implications of which the start-up entrepreneur needs to be aware. However, since it's a good idea to at least provide a brief overview of these matters, I asked for input from two lawyers working with well-known life science firms that have dedicated a lot of legal resources to, and have a lot of experience in, this marketplace.

Chapter 1, contributed by Gerard P. O'Connor of Saul Ewing, identifies the federal and state regulatory bodies, issues that face investors, deal terms, dilution, alternatives to venture capital (VC), and some fundamental company structuring for the new fundraising landscape. Chapter 2, which was written by Robert H. Cohen, a partner in the law firm of McDermott Will

& Emery LLP, and his colleagues, provides further elaboration and insight on the process of raising capital via crowdfunding and IPOs. This content is merely meant to get you thinking; as you will be reminded throughout the book, you must never take any contractual actions without consulting an attorney. Additionally, always remember that whenever you are raising public funds, you will first need to check whether your methodology requires registration with the Securities and Exchange Commission (SEC) and Financial Industry Regulatory Authority (FINRA), as these two entities are responsible for oversight of these processes.

CHAPTER 1

The Legal Landscape— A Basic Overview

Gerard P. O'Connor, Esq.

The face of early stage life science investment is changing. Alternative investors, such as family offices, endowments, foundations, hedge funds, mid-level private equity firms, and angel syndicates, are participating in the space with greater frequency as alternatives to the classic venture capital (VC) funding model. In the face of this evolution in early stage life science funding, entrepreneurs need to be aware of the various legal and regulatory matters that govern the capital-raising process. In this chapter, I will provide you with a brief overview of the more noteworthy of these matters. The information presented is not intended to, nor does it, constitute legal advice. Rather, my purpose is to convey general information across a broad range of topics relevant to raising capital and highlight important issues that you should be aware of as you build your business. The business of offering and selling securities is always evolving, and the laws and regulations surrounding such offerings are currently undergoing intense revision and updating by federal and state regulators. If you are an entrepreneur in the life science space, I advise you to seek appropriate legal counsel to discuss how these complex matters relate to your individual circumstances. The consequences of noncompliance—such as regulatory action and investor lawsuits—can be harsh, even fatal, especially for start-ups with little margin for error in any aspect of their business.

The Players

The process of raising capital by selling equity shares in your company is regulated at both the federal and state levels, with the most important regulatory body being the U.S. Securities and Exchange Commission (SEC). For some offerings that use a financial intermediary, such as an investment banker, the Financial Industry Regulatory Authority (FINRA), formerly known as the National Association of Securities Dealers (NASD), may also play a role. In addition, the state securities regulatory authorities in any state in which the company is offering or selling securities may also play a role. The SEC is charged with interpreting, administering, and promulgating rules under the two main securities laws: the Securities Act of 1933 and the Securities Exchange Act of 1934. These laws have been around for decades and are, depending on your perspective, either mainstays that have provided the foundation for generations of economic vitality and growth or a set of Depression-era relics that have outlived their usefulness. The past two years have been marked by considerable anticipation of major modernizations in federal securities laws, but the pace of real evolution of these laws continues to be measured at best.

Generally speaking, disclosure—telling your investors about not only the opportunity but also the material risks involved with an investment in your company—is the primary focus of federal and state securities law. Simply stated, issuers get into trouble not because their companies and ideas fail but because unhappy investors claim that they were not told the truth about the specific risks. One way to attempt to make the right disclosure is to register the offering with the federal and appropriate state securities regulators, filing a prospectus, providing voluminous disclosure, and responding to comments and questions of the regulators before engaging in the sales process. Federal and state securities laws generally require that securities offerings be registered unless certain exemptions are available. Registration works for large transactions such as IPOs, but it is far too time-consuming and expensive for early stage companies. Therefore, as a practical matter, start-ups must find the appropriate exemption from the registration requirement.

The most common exemption is available via a so-called private placement exemption under Section 4(a)(2) of the Securities Act of 1933, which provides that transactions "not involving a public offering" are exempt from registration. In particular, Rule 506 under Regulation D of the Securities Act provides a safe harbor so that issuers meeting its requirements know that their transaction will be exempt. This safe harbor provides a number of advantages: for one, it permits the issuer to sell shares to an unlimited number of "accredited investors" and not more than 35 nonaccredited investors. Better yet, it preempts state securities laws: if you qualify for the Rule 506 exemption, then you do not have to worry about complying with substantive state laws requiring registration or exemptions but merely have to pay fees and provide copies of the federal filings and other routine documentation. This makes it a lot easier to complete the financing round. In practice, virtually every funding deal with a U.S.-based venture capital (VC) firm, family office, strategic partner, or other institutional investor is exempt under the Rule 506 safe harbor.

You should seek the advice of counsel when examining the exclusions available under the Securities Act, as the penalties of noncompliance can be quite onerous.

Accredited and Nonaccredited Investors

Most early stage capital raises are limited to "accredited investors." What is an accredited investor? Generally, an accredited investor is an individual with a net worth, or combined net worth with his or her spouse, of $1 million[1] or a gross income during each of the past two calendar years that exceeds $200,000 (or $300,000 when combined with the annual income of his or her spouse). Additionally, institutional investors, such as corporations, partnerships, trusts, banks, savings and loan associations, insurance companies, and employee benefit plans, may be accredited investors as long as certain dollar thresholds and other requirements are met. Accredited investors also include directors and certain executive officers

---

[1] Since passage of the 2010 Dodd-Frank Act, individuals are no longer entitled to include the value of their primary residence in their net worth in determining their status as an accredited investor. Likewise, the related amount of indebtedness secured by such person's primary residence up to its fair market value is excluded, except to the extent that the residence is "underwater," that is, the mortgage exceeds the value of the residence.

of the company; for example, the president or a vice president in charge of a particular business unit or a director may be an accredited investor even if that natural person does not satisfy the net worth or gross income thresholds noted earlier.[2]

Also, as mentioned earlier, Rule 506 under Regulation D, the preferred exemption, does permit a limited number of nonaccredited investors to participate in a Regulation D offering. However, because of the additional extensive and detailed information required, this almost never happens in practice.

Some offerings do include nonaccredited investors, by necessity or choice. For example, an initial seed round might include founders as well as friends and family investors who might not qualify as accredited investors. You can successfully create an offering to these investors, but the information requirements are more significant and you should make sure that each investor can properly assess the risk and can afford to sustain the loss of his or her entire investment. Also, having nonaccredited stockholders can make the sale of your company a more cumbersome and expensive process if the buyer wants to acquire your company in a stock-for-stock deal. The buyer will be offering securities to your nonaccredited investors and will have to comply with the additional disclosure requirements. You should consult with legal counsel and carefully weigh the pros and cons, both present and future, of offering securities to nonaccredited investors.

Terms of the Deal

Once you have determined the type of offering you are seeking to conduct, and the type of investors to whom you wish to offer securities, you need to determine the form and terms of your securities offering.

In structuring an early stage offering, one critical variable is the pre-money value of the company (see "A Word About Dilution"). At the ini-

---

[2] Start-ups are sometimes tempted to "pack" the list of "executive officers" in order to ease regulatory hurdles. Directors and officers should be appointed for bona fide purposes, not merely to escape the reach of securities laws.

tial stages, the company often lacks credible indicia of value, making it difficult for the company and the investor to agree. If the valuation is too high, the investor will perceive an insufficient return on a very risky investment and will reject the deal. If it is too low, the company is giving up too much equity.

Convertible notes can help solve this problem. In a convertible note transaction, the investor makes the investment in the form of debt and agrees to convert the debt into equity securities in a later round, usually at a discount and subject to a "conversion cap," or upper limit on the conversion valuation, to protect the investor. Convertible note deals can be comparatively easy to structure and efficient to close, and they offer an alternative to a dilutive equity round early on. However, companies need to consult their advisors both as to the terms of the conversion (which can be surprisingly dilutive to the founders, especially with a conversion) as well as issues relating to interest and tax reporting that accompany these deals. Some companies and their advisors are experimenting with classes of preferred stock that carry the economic attributes of convertible notes but are not classified as debt and do not trigger interest issues.

If the company can agree with the investor as to the pre-money valuation of the company, then usually an equity deal makes the most sense. There are two main forms of early stage equity transactions: the company-led "private placement memorandum" model and the investor-led negotiated term sheet and set of preferred stock closing documents. A private placement memorandum, or PPM, is more commonly used when an intermediary is involved and is usually used for investors who are not likely to demand control over the process or extensive post-closing investor protections. In general, the PPM should contain biographical information relating to key executives, a description of the company's business model, technology, and competitive attributes, as well as information about the risks of investing in the company. In drafting an effective PPM, the company should try to make full and fair disclosure of the company's opportunity and risks, even while protecting proprietary matters that a manager may wish to keep confidential (for example, the company's core technology). You should carefully track copies of the PPM and make sure that it goes only to selected investors. A well-drafted PPM that discloses all the material risks and factors will help to protect the company from later claims.

The investor-led term sheet, with extensive investor-led due diligence and a full set of investment documents, is used by venture capital firms and more sophisticated angel investors and alternative investors. The National Venture Capital Association has developed a set of model documents,[3] which are used for most equity deals led by top-tier VC firms and are increasingly prevalent across the board with a wide variety of angel groups and individual investors.

A Word About Dilution

Dilution may be the most feared aspect of early stage capital raising and may also be the least well understood. Nonetheless, fear of being diluted hinders early stage investors from investing in life science start-ups, especially when it appears that the company will need significant additional equity before becoming cash-flow positive. As an entrepreneur, you should remember that dilution is what you are trying for. You start with 100% (less any cut that a university licensing you the technology might take), and someday, when the company is sold, you'll have zero. The real question is how much dilution is appropriate at any given stage? In an early stage offering, the biggest questions are:

- What is the company worth now?
- How much money does the company need at this stage of development?
- What milestone is the company going to achieve with the funds?
- How much will the valuation increase as a result?

One easy way to think of this matrix of factors is that the percentage that the investors will hold will be equal to (a) the number of dollars they invest divided by (b) the total "post-money valuation," (that is, the pre-money valuation plus the dollars raised in the offering), as illustrated in Figure 1.1.

---

[3] See http://www.nvca.org/index.php?option=com_content&view=article&id=108&Itemid=136 for the set of model documents.

Pre-Money Valuation:	$4,000,000
Amount Raised:	$1,000,000
Total Post-Deal Value:	$5,000,000
Percent Owned by Investors:	20%
Everything Else:	80%

FIGURE 1.1: *Breaking down a valuation*

"Everything else" includes not only all founders' stock, friends and family shares, and any options issued before the transaction but also typically includes an option pool of between 10% and 20% of the total equity. Thus, the pre-money valuation is a critical factor, as it is the primary determinant of how much of the company the founders will own after the transaction. Other factors also affect the post-deal founders' share. In the example, assume that the company is raising $2,000,000 instead of $1,000,000 and that the investors are requiring a post-closing option pool of 20% in order to attract and retain a management team. Now, the investors get 33% of the company, and after subtracting the 20% option pool, the founders' stake has gone from 80% to 47% on a "fully diluted basis," meaning including all issuable shares under options, etc. as if they were already issued. But increase the valuation from $4,000,000 to $6,000,000 and the same deal leaves the founders with 55%.

Dilution is a key component of evaluating the deal for an entrepreneur, as it affects both the economic relationship among the stakeholders and control of the company. A common fallacy is the idea that the founders need to retain a majority of the issued and outstanding shares on a fully diluted basis. In reality, this is cold comfort, because professional investors will invariably require a number of control and veto rights that attach to their preferred stock, so your ownership of an outright majority is not as meaningful as you might think. The better approach is to review the documents carefully. Are there appropriate checks and balances on the investors' control? More importantly, what is the imputed value of the founders' shares after the transaction? If it is increasing, then dilution is working the right way from that standpoint.

You need to work with experienced legal and financial advisors to understand the type of dilution and control risks that you and other early stage investors face, to interpret and negotiate the various provisions of the deal documents that can affect dilution, and to model dilution accurately on a pro forma basis. Dilution is a necessary and even desirable aspect of fundraising, but you need to be aware of its effect so that you can raise the right amount of money, at the right time, and at a valuation that fairly reflects both the company's value and the risk being taken by the investor.

Alternatives to Venture Capital

The traditional VC path in the life science space appears to be under stress. Many industry observers proclaim that life science VC is a broken model and no longer able to achieve required returns for the venture fund limited partners. Some stalwarts maintain that life science VC actually outperforms other sectors of the VC asset class. Whoever is right, the fact is that there are a growing number of alternatives to traditional VC of which every early stage life science entrepreneur should be aware. In the rapidly evolving life science space, with several different models emerging, finding the right funding partner is becoming an increasingly complex task.

Some of the more attractive alternatives include:

- **Corporate VC.** Large pharmaceutical and other companies may make good investment partners. Corporate venture capitalists can add a strategic fit in terms of therapeutic or diagnostic and can provide significant assistance in clinical strategy. Entrepreneurs need to choose a corporate VC partner with care. The entrepreneur is likely to be attached to the partner, for better or for worse, whereas the corporate venture capitalist may change strategic direction or simply make new budget priorities.

- **Venture philanthropy.** Foundations and family offices with a focus on specific diseases or research paths are increasingly emerging in the life science space. Foundations can provide funding ranging from grants to milestone development payments to terms that resemble standard VC-preferred stock deals. Foundations are mission driven, not purely bottom-line driven, so they may be seen by entrepreneurs as more dependable than corporate partners over the long haul.

- **Government funding.** NIH funding is non-dilutive and plentiful: NIH provided over $630 million in Small Business Innovation Research (SBIR) funding in fiscal year 2012.[4] If you take SBIR funding, you will become subject to special government accounting and audit requirements. SBIR awards are typically capped at $150,000 for phase I awards and $1,000,000 for phase II awards.

General Solicitation

For 80 years, the biggest rule to remember in conducting a private placement of securities was that the offering process could not involve any "general solicitation," meaning advertisements, notices, articles, TV, radio, and other forms of mass communication. In 1933, the idea of what constituted a "general solicitation" was fairly clear. Over the years, though, methods of mass communication have proliferated greatly. Also, today's start-ups find ever more investor conferences, business incubators, and other opportunities to present their case. Participation in these events may constitute "general solicitation" under the law.

In September 2013, the SEC finalized a rule, required by the Jumpstart Our Business Startups (JOBS) Act, permitting general solicitation in certain cases. At first glance, it seemed that this new rule would quickly make it easier for start-ups to raise funds by advertising on the company's website, sending out emails, tweeting on the company's Twitter account, etc. However, it has not been that simple, and so far, the new rule has not really opened up access to capital in the way that was envisioned by its congressional sponsors. First, the rule requires that in a deal with general solicitation, not only must all of the purchasers of the securities be accredited

---

[4] Source: "Small Business Innovation Research (SBIR) and Small Business Technology Transfer (SBTT) Programs," National Institutes of Health website, last modified March 6, 2013, http://grants.nih.gov/grants/funding/sbirsttr_programs.htm.

investors (as is common in any Rule 506 deal) but also that the issuer must take reasonable steps to "verify" that the purchasers of the securities are accredited investors. This step of "verification" has met with some resistance among the community of angel investors that should be the natural targets of general solicitations. Investors have objected to the idea of providing tax returns or other personal information in order to verify accredited investor status.

Also, the new attention to the issue of general solicitation has, ironically, focused attention on types of general solicitation that used to fall through the cracks. Start-ups as well as federal and state regulators have long ignored the general solicitation rule as it applied to pitches made at business plan competitions and industry conferences. Now, due to increased attention, start-ups are being importuned to make sure that their presentations do not constitute a solicitation of interest in an investment (though it is hard to imagine why else these companies would be pitching at a business plan competition in the first place). So, paradoxically, the statutory removal of the ban on general solicitation has, so far, created more complications than it has removed. Hopefully, the angel investment community will find some way to get comfortable with verifying accredited investor status, and issuers will be able to expand their reach into the investor community, as the JOBS Act intended.

A Word About Brokers and Finders

Launching and growing a company is a full-time entrepreneurial endeavor, and raising capital can be a specialized skill. Founders of life science start-ups, consumed with building their company and achieving technical milestones, frequently turn to third parties to help find investors. You should be aware, though, that accepting these services may raise certain regulatory concerns. The business of finding investors for early stage companies requires licensure as a broker or investment adviser on both the federal and state levels. If you use an unlicensed broker or finder to sell securities, then you may be subject to regulatory sanctions, including offering rescission to investors who were so solicited. Self-described "finders" without licenses proliferate in the start-up community. Many of these individuals insist that their work is legal, that they have been doing it for a long time, and/or that they are not subject to license requirements because they are not negotiating deal terms, or because they are acting as a "finder" only, or because they maintain some paper relationship with a licensed broker to provide "clearing" services. These rationales are usually wrong. If you are approached by an unlicensed individual offering services to help you find investors, be wary and seek the advice of qualified securities counsel before proceeding.

Structuring the Company to Meet the New Funding Environment

In addition to selecting the right funding from the right partner on the right terms, a successful life science entrepreneur can form and grow the company to better utilize smaller-sized, less dilutive financing rounds. "Virtual" companies can stay small and efficient by outsourcing functions from financial to clinical activities; using incubator space that is shorter term and more flexible (this also sometimes comes with access to laboratory facilities); and using contract work instead of hiring full-time employees. To operate successfully in a virtual environment, you need to assess and deal with a wide range of legal issues, including:

- Employment and independent contractor laws respecting early team members
- Privacy laws and regulations that might apply to your clinical and user information
- Intellectual property, nondisclosure, and competition issues that arise in contracted services agreements

Summary

In conclusion, this is an exciting time to be in the early stage market. Current market circumstances stand to reward the entrepreneur who can assess and exploit the legal risks and opportunities successfully. You should be sure to stay apprised of the opportunities offered by these emerging legal realities; don't overstate the opportunity and/or understate the risks involved, but rather provide your investors with full and fair disclosure of the facts material to their investment decision. Be aware of new means of offering securities and alternative investor classes, but also remember that the best solution for one company might not work for another. Obtain good counsel from legal, tax, and accounting professionals and incorporate that counsel into your business plan. And finally, learn and use best practices relating to your business. They may or may not be legally required, but are increasingly recognized, and demanded, by both institutional and individual investors.

৯৹৶

Gerard O'Connor's practice focuses on business matters ranging from mergers and acquisitions and corporate finance to intellectual property. He represents clients in a variety of industries, including life sciences, clean energy technology, renewable energy, venture capital, and professional services.

Gerard's experience includes representing buyers and sellers of public and private companies and assisting early stage companies with formation, securities offerings, employment, and intellectual property issues. He also counsels public companies and their directors and officers on securities law, Sarbanes-Oxley compliance, and reporting obligations.

CHAPTER 2

The Legal Landscape— Crowdfunding and IPOs

Robert H. Cohen, Esq.

In this chapter, we will provide you with a brief overview of the legal process for a life science company that is considering raising equity capital through public investors. More specifically, we will focus on the process of raising such capital through crowdfunding and initial public offerings (IPOs). This information is not intended to be, nor does it constitute, legal advice. Instead, our purpose is to provide context and background to assist you in making future equity capital-raising decisions as you grow your business. Primarily due to the Jumpstart Our Business Startups (JOBS) Act, the laws and regulations surrounding capital raises for emerging growth companies (EGCs) have been, and may continue to be, subject to change. If you are contemplating, or are currently in the process of, raising equity capital through an IPO, crowdfunding, or other public source of equity capital, we advise you to seek legal counsel to discuss how any of the issues covered in this chapter might relate to your individual circumstances.

First and foremost, for a life science company considering an equity capital raise of public funds, the most important step for each party involved, whether such party is the company, the bank or underwriter, the agent, and/or the investor, is ensuring both that the intellectual property (IP) of the company is sufficiently protected by valid, enforceable patents and that the IP will remain protected for a substantial (or long enough) period of time. Additionally, the parties will be concerned with the remaining shelf life of the company's existing IP, and this may impact how much pressure the company is faced with to expand on its existing IP.

Crowdfunding

Since the passage of the JOBS Act, the financial and medical press has anticipated the potential for crowdfunding to revolutionize fundraising for early stage life science companies. Recently, a portal exclusively dedicated to crowdfunding life science and healthcare start-ups launched at Medstartr.com. Although crowdfunding may present an exciting opportunity for your company, this approach has both its limitations and risks.

Models

There are two distinct crowdfunding models. The first is the donation model exemplified by existing portals such as Kickstarter.com. Portals adhering to the donation model post interesting projects, for which individuals then donate largely unlimited sums for no return or, at most, access to discounts or early release of a project's product. The second model, and the type that the Securities and Exchange Commission (SEC) is tasked with regulating, is an equity-based or investment-based model, which involves an actual investment in an entity that is pursuing the project. Members of the "crowd" that provide funding to the project receive an ownership interest in the entity. This investment model has been highly anticipated by life science investors since it was first authorized in the U.S. under the JOBS Act in 2011. On October 23, 2013, the SEC released its proposed regulations establishing equity crowdfunding. As of this writing, the SEC is seeking public comment on the proposed rules for a 90-day period before determining whether to adopt them and release the final regulations.

Access to Markets

Companies that seek to use investment-based crowdfunding will not be permitted to send out mass solicitations at will. Equity-based crowdfunding must take place only through brokers or portals that are registered with the SEC; such brokers and portals are a new class of SEC registrant. In addition to registering with the SEC, equity portals will be responsible for conducting due diligence on potential investments, including background checks on directors and executive officers of the company. The portals that are currently active, such as Kickstarter.com, Medstartr.com, and Indiegogo.com, are not equity-based portals but donation portals. The SEC is not involved in regulating such donation portals because the donors do not receive any equity in return for their donations.

Access to Capital

Under the JOBS Act, the aggregate amount of interests sold to equity investors through an investment-based portal in any 12-month period may not exceed $1 million. Individual investors will also have caps placed on their equity investments of (a) the greater of $2,000 or 5% of the annual income or net worth of the investor, as applicable, if either the annual income or the net worth of the investor is less than $100,000 or (b) 10% of the annual income or net worth of an investor, as applicable, if either the annual income or net worth of the investor is equal to or greater than $100,000. In no event may an individual investor exceed a maximum aggregate investment of $100,000. Given the extremely high costs of clinical trials, equipment, and supplies in the life science industry, these investment caps may prove to be too limiting to add any real value to start-up companies interested in investment-based crowdfunding, especially given the added regulatory hurdles involved in the equity-raising process.

However, due in part to the broker registration costs and due diligence requirements imposed on brokers, it is expected that the fees charged by approved portals may be upward of 10% to 20% of the total amount raised. This exceeds the 3% to 5% fee typically charged by broker-dealers in a registered offering and the 6% to 10% fee typically charged by investment banks running an IPO. Crowdfunding through a licensed platform may therefore be an extremely expensive way to raise what is ultimately a relatively limited and finite amount of equity capital. However, entrepreneurs of some companies that would not otherwise have access to these funds may not view these limitations as a "deal killer."

Regulatory Hurdles

If a company raises between $100,000 and $500,000 through an equity crowdfunding portal, the JOBS Act requires the company to have its financial statements *reviewed* by an independent certified public accountant, and if the company raises over $500,000, the company is required to have its financial statements *audited* by an independent certified public accountant. Reviewed and audited financial statements are costly and are not typically included in the budget for start-up companies raising less than $1 million. Additionally, the company must draft an informational memorandum and file this informational memorandum with the SEC prior to the launch of the crowdfunding offering. Once the offering is concluded, the company (or issuer) will be required to annually file with the SEC and provide its investors with reports of the results of operations and financial statements, as the SEC deems appropriate. These are extraordinarily burdensome regulatory obligations for start-up companies to comply with, particularly if less than $1 million is raised through a crowdfunding offering.

In addition to the financial statement requirements, the SEC has proposed that a company seeking to raise funds through equity crowdfunding would, among other things, be required in its offering documents to disclose:

- Information about officers and directors, as well as owners of 20% or more of the company
- A description of the company's business and the use of proceeds from the offering
- The price to the public of the securities being offered, the target offering amount, the deadline to reach the target offering amount, and whether the company will accept investments in excess of the target offering amount
- Certain related-party transactions
- A description of the financial condition of the company

Confidentiality

Life science companies are extremely competitive, often possessing sensitive and proprietary information that they want to maintain privately. Crowdfunding portals and the information requirements established by the JOBS

Act will require disclosures (such as those noted earlier) from early stage life science companies. Having a large number of shareholders after a successful crowdfunding campaign will further threaten a company's ability to keep its information confidential because of the difficulty in regulating the flow of information after it has been released to shareholders.

Future Funding

If a company is successful in raising funds through a crowdfunding portal, it may create future issues with the company's capitalization table. Having 25, 50, or even possibly 1,000 shareholders in a start-up entity can create serious practical and administrative issues for raising the next round of capital, as many state corporation laws provide shareholders with protections such as approval rights over certain actions, one of which may be funding through additional investors. Getting large numbers of shareholders to approve a future round of funding may be so difficult and cumbersome that it may ultimately threaten the long-term viability of the company. Many venture capitalists avoid crowdfunded companies due to the potential problems in obtaining approval for subsequent funding rounds.

Regulation D

Aside from crowdfunding, there is one type of change that has officially arrived for early stage corporate funding. Changes to Regulation D Rule 506 have loosened restrictions on publicizing private offerings. This will allow companies to advertise more openly to investors, such as on patient advocacy websites or even in magazines and newspapers. Unlike with equity crowdfunding, Rule 506 investors must be "Accredited Investors" (for an individual this means having an annual income over $200,000 [or $300,000 when combined with the annual income of his or her spouse] in each of the two most recent years or having at least $1 million in assets, excluding the value of the individual's primary residence). Additionally, institutional investors, such as corporations, partnerships, trusts, banks, savings and loan associations, insurance companies, and employee benefit plans, may be accredited investors as long as certain dollar thresholds and other requirements are met. Significantly, unlike the limits placed on equity crowdfunding portals, a Regulation D Rule 506 offering does not limit the amount of equity raised.

Initial Public Offering

Regulators

If you are in the mid to late stages of capital raising, you may be interested in transforming your life science company from a private to a public one, through an IPO. In addition to filing your offering with the Financial Industry Regulatory Authority (FINRA) and the SEC to have your shares traded after your IPO, you will need to have your shares registered and listed on a national exchange, typically either the New York Stock Exchange (NYSE) or the NASDAQ Stock Market (NASDAQ), or registered and quoted on an over-the-counter (OTC) bulletin board or marketplace. NYSE and NAS-DAQ have similar, but not identical, listing requirements, including minimum equity and market value of shares requirements, as well as ongoing corporate governance and other requirements for your company once you have completed your IPO. The OTC has much less stringent eligibility requirements for quoting securities, which are essentially limited to having registered the shares with the SEC; however, the OTC has significant limitations on trading activity as compared to a national exchange.

Securities

The security that is most commonly offered to public investors in an IPO is "common stock." The rights and privileges of common stockholders are set in the company's charter, which is filed in its jurisdiction of incorporation. However, other types of securities may be offered, either in conjunction with one another or alone. These include (i) warrants, which are usually exercisable to purchase common stock at a certain set price, (ii) units, which are a combination of multiple securities, and (iii) preferred stock, which is similar to common stock but has certain distinguishing rights, often related to voting rights or shareholder protections.

When considering an IPO, an important question aside from how much capital you want to raise is what percentage of your company do you want to sell? Or put another way, how much of your company do you want to retain? One way to maintain control over your company after selling shares to the public is to retain preferred stock with voting rights that results in treatment of the preferred stockholder as a majority shareholder. Another way would be to sell only a small percentage of the outstanding shares, such as between 20% and 50%. Maintaining such control has the added benefit of providing your company with an exemption from some of the myriad corporate governance and other requirements imposed by national exchanges after the completion of an IPO (as noted earlier). If your company remains a "controlled company," which means a company in which more than 50% of the voting power for the election of directors is held by an individual, a defined and disclosed group, or another company, your company will be exempt from certain of these ongoing requirements, including the requirement to have a board of directors composed of a majority of independent directors.

Offering Process

So you have decided to undergo an IPO. Assuming you are a U.S.-based entity, you will prepare and file a Form S-1 registration statement with the SEC (foreign corporations would use a Form F-1). Historically, the filing process entailed publicly filing your registration statement with the SEC from the outset, allowing the public and your competitors to know your plans and see your disclosures at this early stage. The JOBS Act has changed this equation. Now an EGC, defined as any issuer that had total annual gross revenues of less than $1 billion during its most recently completed fiscal year, can initially submit confidential draft registration statements to the SEC and go through the comment letter and response process outside the public eye. While any and all confidential draft registration statements will become public information as soon as you publicly file a Form S-1 registration statement (which as a rule must be at least 21 days prior to the commencement of your road show for the offering), the ability to handle the SEC review process behind the scenes allows you to delay publicly disclosing your position to competitors and affords you a level of confidentiality should you decide to abandon the IPO prior to publicly filing.

There are many fees involved in an IPO, such as registration fees to each of the SEC and FINRA, which are based on the maximum aggregate offering price (total number of shares offered multiplied by the per-share price of the shares). You will also pay an initial listing fee (and subsequently pay continued listing fees) to the exchange on which your company is listed. There will be legal, accounting, printing, road show, travel, insurance, indemnification, and other miscellaneous expenses. But the largest up-front expense will generally be the underwriting commission. The under-writers will generally command anywhere from 6% to 10% of the offering proceeds, in addition to other negotiated fee reimbursements.

Federal securities laws impact the ability of a company undergoing an IPO and its employees and representatives to make public statements or other communications during the periods prior to and following the filing of a registration statement. The SEC has been vigilant in addressing perceived violations of these legal requirements (see Figure 2.1 and Figure 2.2).

Generally Permissible	Generally Impermissible
1. Dissemination of information about products and services, including:	1. Any publicity intended to or likely to stimulate investor or dealer interest in the company or its stock
a. Product and service advertisements consistent with past practices	2. Issuing forecasts, projections, or predictions or opinions concerning valuation, revenues, earnings, etc.
b. Factual information on business developments (e.g., press release regarding the acquisition of additional properties) consistent with past practices	3. Distributing written material relating to the company's business (except factual information distributed in the ordinary course and consistent with past practice and previously used product advertising)
c. Technical articles in the technical press	4. Any significant increase in product and services advertisements or promotion without review of counsel
2. Stockholders' meetings—answering factual questions from stockholders	5. Interviews, speeches, and articles in the popular press
3. Announcement of intention to file (if in accordance with SEC Rule 135)	6. Discussions with analysts or stockholders except for unsolicited inquiries regarding factual matters consistent with past practices
	7. Adding new information regarding the company (other than factual matters consistent with past practices) or its securities to the company's website
	8. Posting informatin about the company (other than factual matters consistent with past practices) or its securities on social media

FIGURE 2.1: *Rules regarding communications before public filing of the registration statement*

Generally Permissible	Generally Impermissible
1. Items 1 and 2 above	1. Distributing any written materials with the preliminary prospectus (unless free writing prospectus approved by working group and in accordance with all applicable SEC rules including any filing requirements)
2. Distributing preliminary prospectuses	2. Distributing (or assisting others to distribute) any written materials intended or likely to stimulate investor or dealer interest in the company or the stock
3. Making oral statements about the company or oral "offers" of the stock	3. Making oral statements or "offers" to potential investors that violate the "antifraud" provisions of the law (or selectively disclosing information not generally available to all investors in the preliminary prospectus)

FIGURE 2.2: *Rules regarding communications after filing and before effectiveness of the registration statement (waiting period)*

Testing the Waters

The JOBS Act expanded permissible communications by EGCs by permitting an EGC, or any person authorized to act on behalf of an EGC, either before or after the filing of a registration statement, to "test the waters" by engaging in oral or written communications with potential investors that are qualified institutional buyers or institutions that are accredited investors to determine whether such investors might have an interest in a contemplated securities offering.

Typical water-testing activities may resemble a road show presentation where management and the underwriters meet with potential investors and give a presentation describing the company and the proposed offering. Because the anti-fraud provisions of the Securities Act still apply, water-testing presentations should be vetted with counsel and should be prepared with the same degree of diligence as a traditional road show presentation. Additionally, it should be expected that during an SEC review of the company's registration statement, the SEC likely will request a description of any water-testing activities and will request copies of any materials that were provided in connection with such activities.

Summary

Both crowdfunding and IPOs can be effective strategies for growing your company and helping move it forward to the next phase of its development.[5] One is a relatively new, untested method, and the other has been undertaken by many companies, providing countless examples you can research and learn from. Strongly consider the pros and cons of each, as well as where you are in the timeline of your company, and of course, always retain legal counsel before taking any steps to raise public funds, as the regulatory burden is high and any illegal action, even unknowingly taken, could be detrimental for you and for your company.

ଓଡ଼

Robert H. Cohen is a partner in McDermott Will & Emery's Corporate Department. He focuses his practice on transactional and securities work for a broad range of clients, including initial and follow-on public offerings, registered direct and PIPE financings, private placements, bridge financings, and equity line and reverse mergers. Bob has extensive experience in the areas of mergers and acquisitions, joint ventures, 1933 and 1944 Act representation, and licensing and distribution arrangements. From his years of experience, Bob has developed industry-specific knowledge across numerous markets, particularly in the life science industry, having represented the financing and mergers and acquisitions activity for pharmaceutical and medical device companies.

---

[5] Please feel free to contact us for a copy of *The IPO and Public Company Primer: A Practical Guide to Going Public, Raising Capital and Life as a Public Company*. Coauthored by McDermott partners David Cifrino, Tom Conaghan, and Tom Murphy, this 350-page guide provides detailed information about the IPO process, including the significant changes to the IPO process made by the JOBS Act, and being a public company. You can also get a copy from our website at http://www.mwe.com/files/Uploads/Documents/Pubs/The-IPO-and-Public-Company-Primer.pdf.

Finding Investor Candidates That Are a Fit for Your Firm

CHAPTER 3

Going It Alone or Choosing a Fundraising Partner

Every entrepreneur in the life science field who is seeking to raise capital must make a decision at some point about whether to do so using a fundraising partner. On the surface, the answer seems obvious—let an expert who has experience in such matters handle it so others on the team can concentrate on their areas of expertise. However, the arena of early stage fundraising partners is filled with a diverse cast of characters that constitute a "Wild West" of sorts. The purpose of this chapter is to provide you with some insight as to why a fundraising partner may or may not make sense for your company and to examine the various forms these fundraising partners take along with their respective advantages and disadvantages.

The first thing every fundraising executive needs to do is look in the mirror and determine whether he or she has what it takes to go outbound. As we go into the nitty-gritty of exactly what it means to embark on a fundraising campaign, you need to ask yourself whether you have the capacity to create the necessary materials, compile the investor list, and stay on the task of managing outbound mailings, conducting the 30 to 40 daily follow-up calls, and scheduling the meetings. Simply put, some have what it takes and others do not. Some of us are preprogrammed for this kind of activity. If it's beyond your ability or you just don't have any experience with it, you have to ask yourself whether you want to learn how to do it. As is true with other challenging endeavors, you will only succeed in mastering all the facets of outbound fundraising if you have a strong inner desire to do so.

Marketing and lab science really aren't so dissimilar when it comes to the numbers involved. Experimental science and marketing are both based on very high failure rates—failure is innate in both of these sciences! Yes, I just stated that marketing is a science. The rates of success are similar; you have to try something 100 times before getting one or two positives. The same mind-set required in the lab must be applied to outbound marketing: you must delight in irregular wins, despite the inevitably high failure rates. Both require individuals who can persevere day to day under these adverse circumstances. That is precisely what makes a great scientist and a great marketer.

To start to develop an investor relationship, someone has to take a list of investor candidates, reach out to them, and set up meetings. This simple act is a lot harder than it sounds because every start-up is trying to talk to the same investor candidates. It is a tedious job and you have to be incredibly persistent in navigating around all the barriers that are out there.

The first big question to answer is who is going to be the point person for owning the outbound efforts needed to secure investor meetings? Let's take a quick look at the decision tree regarding this pivotal strategy (see Figure 3.1). The first and best choice is that you, the leader of your company, decides to bite the bullet and learn a new set of skills in order to go out and find the capital. If this is impossible, can someone else in your organization manage this task effectively and willingly? Your last option should be to go with a third-party entity only if there is no possibility of a member of your company devoting the time and resources to outreach.

Remember that even if you choose an outside partner, you and your team are still going to be hitting the road to attend meetings; make no mistake about that fact. Somebody in-house has to own the outbound aspect of outreach to investor candidates and be actively involved in the process of courting them. You can outsource some of the specific tasks, but you still need in-house ownership of the process.

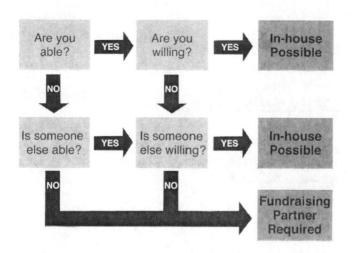

FIGURE 3.1: *Deciding whether or not to use a fundraising partner*

No matter who sets up the meeting, the executive team must sell the company and innovation or product to the investors. There is no way to get around that fact. Simply put, investors invest in companies—the people and the products. Having a sound management team is as important as having a great product—that is a nonnegotiable fact of fundraising.

Engaging with Broker-Dealers

In the United States, anyone engaged in the business of facilitating a purchase or sale of securities between a buyer and a seller is required to be a registered "broker-dealer" (see Figure 3.2). This registration is governed by the Securities and Exchange Commission (SEC) of the U.S. government and the Financial Industry Regulatory Authority (FINRA). Most states also regulate broker-dealers under separate state securities laws. Regulatory climates are different in other parts of the world, but generally speaking, most countries have a regulatory framework surrounding these types of transactions.

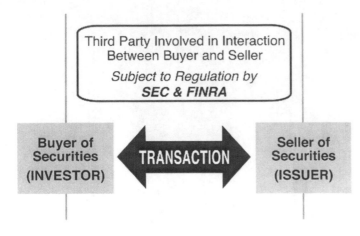

FIGURE 3.2: *Operational environments of third parties*

Being registered essentially means that these firms have agreed to meet certain compliance standards, have vetted their staff and ensured that staff members have passed certain license examinations, and have been officially cleared to engage in raising money and selling securities. Unfortunately there are also many unregistered entities that engage in raising money without meeting these regulatory standards. Let it be said that this book is not a source of any legal advice and that you should always consult with your legal expert before engaging in business with any fundraising partner.

Categories of Fundraising Partners

So what exactly is a fundraising partner? It's a broad, catch-all term for any-one who claims to have the ability to raise capital for you through his or her investor network. Within this general definition are dozens of models, ranging from the highly sophisticated investment banks to the "friend-of-a-friend" sourcers and finders (whom I will describe in detail later in this chapter). Wherever there is a thriving market rich with start-ups, you will find the third-party service providers that will match up those companies with capital. Where there is tremendous upside and opportunity, everyone and his brother wants to cash in on the next big thing, so many entities jockey for position as the go-to guys who can find the capital and bring companies to the right investor. Navigating this third-party fundraising market can be difficult even for an expert, let alone a novice.

The main challenge when raising funds is understanding what is legal and what isn't. Unfortunately, determining this is going to cost you money, as you need a lawyer to advise you on these matters, since the rules and regulations are ever changing. Other considerations are how much these third parties charge you, what the company promises to deliver, and what they expect you to give in return. Key details to remember are that it is the executive team and the strength of their product that will ultimately convince the investor on the decision to allocate and that all the heavy lifting will be done by your team during the vetting and product due diligence processes. You must be careful not to give away too much for introductions and potential relationships, since the brunt of the effort will still fall on you and your team to get a deal done.

Payment methods requested can vary widely. Many third-party entities want a stipend or retainer that can range from a few thousand dollars a month to tens of thousands of dollars. They sometimes want a percentage of the amount they help you raise, which can range from 2% to over 20%. Many of these entities want warrants (a warrant is an option to buy stock at a particular price) as part of the fee deal; still others demand equity (a piece of your company).

Third-party entities tend to gravitate to what is hot and represents the quickest path to a cash payout. Many times these entities have a stable of start-ups they are representing, some of whom naturally capture investor attention more easily than others. These start-ups will always be prioritized, and if you're not one of the top priorities, you may be left in the wings paying a monthly stipend and not getting any investor meetings.

So you can see that when I refer to the third-party fundraising sector as the Wild West, I am not joking! You must have a sophisticated team around you so you can be sure that you are being charged fair industry standard rates and that there is someone to raise the red flag if any terms sound unfavorable. It is very easy to become the victim of a predatory strategy of a convincing third-party entity. Buyer beware!

That being said, there are plenty of upstanding third-party fundraising entities you can work with, and later in the chapter, I will provide you with a guide to help you vet these partners. I have broken these entities into six general categories (see Figure 3.3).

Entity	General Description
The finder or sourcer	Typically an individual with a "strong" network; make sure they have the appropriate licenses to represent you in the buying and selling of equities.
The third-party marketer	Can be an individual or a regional or global firm; sophistication varies. Make sure they have the appropriate licenses to represent you in the buying and selling of equities.
The investor-audience provider	Can be a "connected" individual or firm. Uses a pay-to-present model; be sure to check references for recent success stories.
The consultant or advisor	Typically an individual or small firm; tends to be sophisticated and often offers value-added services.
The investment bank	Can be a firm of any size; tends to be sophisticated and typically offers value-added services.
The crowdfunding portal	A potential solution for very early stage companies; most appear to be a relatively costly option, and their legal status is pending.

FIGURE 3.3: *Types of fundraising partners*

The Finder or Sourcer

This category covers a broad spectrum of entities that claim to have the ability to source capital via special, high-end personal networks. They come in two flavors: sourcers have some technical expertise that allows them to vet deals, so that when they present an opportunity to someone with capital, they can claim to have gone through a first due diligence process of sorts; finders claim to have connections in the "right places" and that they can get you into introductory meetings with people who have money. The "right" places could take the form of a venture capital (VC) firm, family office, or other such established investors. The finders may claim that they are the only access point and that only they possess the inside knowledge required to reach these investors.

Finders and sourcers will often surface at events and conferences that focus on guiding entrepreneurs in fundraising. There are very successful, well-connected sourcers and finders with the right licenses and strong networks that can be excellent and productive resources for entrepreneurs raising money. However, this category also has its share of unlicensed entities that operate in a legal gray zone. As such, it is imperative that an entrepreneur does his or her own due diligence and carefully vets a company or individual before engaging in any sort of agreement. Either of these constituents can charge you for general services or meetings, or get a piece of a deal—or a combination of both.

The Third-Party Marketer

Third-party marketers are firms or individuals that market securities on behalf of your company. They have lists of investors of various types and promote your firm to them in order to source your capital. Simply put, a third-party marketer is an outsourced sales force that helps to sell your equity.

Although there are many registered third-party marketers, some of them are unregistered; you must proceed with extreme caution when negotiating with these entities. The third-party marketers typically are compensated through a monthly retainer plus a success fee in the form of a percentage of the money they raise.

The Investor-Audience Provider

These entities are essentially "pay-to-play" matchmakers that typically charge you a fee to go to a preset meeting with a potential investor or group of investors. When it comes to these types of scenarios, if it sounds too good to be true, then it probably is. There have been stories of these types of arrangements leading to allocations, but simple logic would indicate that a truly serious investor or group of investors who would be interested in the long-term viability of the companies in which they are investing wouldn't want to potentially hamper their development by charging up-front fees just for a first meeting. If investors trust in their investments, they would undoubtedly rather see that money put toward the growth of the company or product.

Anecdotally speaking, many investors with whom my company Life Science Nation (LSN) works have at some point been approached by an investor-audience provider, and the experience has usually proven to be a disappointment.

The Consultant or Advisor

Consultants are an interesting breed in the fundraising space, largely because the term is used so broadly. There are many different kinds of fundraising consultants that utilize a variety of compensation models. However, a consultant could be simply defined as a third-party marketer that offers some insight and expertise on how to approach your capital raise. They are typically individuals or small firms, and though they may not have the arsenal of resources that a full-service investment bank can offer, they can help to some degree with advice on positioning and developing a market strategy.

Consultants can vary in terms of quality and legal legitimacy, so be careful in navigating the territory. Consultants, like third-party marketers, typically are compensated through a monthly retainer or a success fee in the form of a percentage of the money they raise, and sometimes both.

The Investment Bank

Investment banks (or I-banks) are typically certified broker-dealers that have access to life science entrepreneurs and a myriad of investors; some specialize in high–net-worth individuals, family offices, and institutional connections. Though there is considerable crossover between I-banks and third-party marketers, one of the primary differentiators is that I-banks often offer strategic advisory services. Additionally, they often compose the offering memorandum and other components of the legal paperwork required in the fundraising round.

To establish a productive relationship with the right I-bank, it is important to undertake a thorough vetting process. You need to find a life science–specialized firm that understands the industry's technology, knows the marketplace, and has access to current life science investor data. At the very least, find an I-bank that is specialized and has access to the right kind of clients. Investment banks, like third-party marketers, are usually compensated through a monthly retainer, plus a success fee (typically about 6%) as a percentage of the money they raise; as with other entities, they can decide to throw in warrants and equity as part of the package as well.

The Crowdfunding Portal

As already discussed in the legal section of this book, crowdfunding potentially represents a new fundraising partner category. The Jumpstart Our Business Startups (JOBS) Act, pending SEC acceptance of the new rules, can allow a fundraising executive to use an online portal to raise money via an online campaign. You may refer to the Crowdfunding section of Chapter 2 for an overview of the current rules and regulations in place for this type of investing, though as of the writing of this book, they are far from established. Again, please ensure that you are up to date on the legal requirements for all fundraising transactions, as they are constantly evolving and changing.

Because there is a ceiling on the amount that can be raised through crowdfunding, it is likely best suited for early stage financing to get a company off the ground. Moreover, the fees associated with these portals are likely to be disproportionately high, as justified by promises of quick and easy money. Additionally, the regulatory compliance work required over the long term, coupled with the large number of investors to whom you will be beholden, could make this a less attractive option. Because it is an untested model, when it comes to equity crowdfunding for life science companies, the proof will be in the pudding.

Regulation D

Changes to Regulation D Rule 506 have done more than opened up the possibility of using crowdfunding as a tool; restrictions have also been loosened on soliciting capital for private offerings. Essentially, Rule 506 implies that it is now legal (though you must review this with an attorney) to solicit private investment capital directly from accredited individual investors (with certain income stipulations—see the Regulation D section of Chapter 2 for more detailed information on this).

This opens an enormous wealth of opportunity to companies seeking to raise money, as these entities could previously only be propositioned with an investment opportunity after certain requirements implying an established and ongoing prior relationship had been met (for example, a history of meetings over a specified period of time). Changes to Rule 506 will lead to a massive reduction in red tape and the compliance work required to raise money. Additionally, fundraising via this avenue doesn't carry with it the same limits on capital that crowdfunding does. In fact, you can raise as much as you'd like, without any formal caps or limits (see Figure 3.4).

This regulatory change is groundbreaking for fundraising executives and offers huge potential if effectively leveraged. It will greatly enhance the ability of my company LSN to assist entrepreneurs in raising capital using an outbound fundraising strategy, as the timeline to cash has been greatly shortened.

Vetting Fundraising Partners

As mentioned in the introduction to this chapter, the landscape of fundraising partners is a veritable Wild West. There are some excellent firms that are trustworthy and have proven track records, but there are many unscrupulous entities with dubious legal or moral standards. I have heard both great reports and terrifying tales regarding every category of fundraising partner, so I know that there is no uniformly standard right choice. However, here are a few questions to help guide your evaluation:

- How many clients is the entity currently working with? Too few, and there may be a reason they are having trouble selling their services. Too many, and they may be taking a shotgun approach, hoping to hit on whatever is hot and potentially leaving you by the wayside.

- Ask about their track record—how much did they charge and help raise? Where, when, for whom, and from whom? If the firm or individual isn't able to elaborate on their last few deals, that's a red flag.

Regulation D, Rule 506 & Crowdfunding Regulatory Overview*

	New Rule 506c Offerings	Crowdfunding (Pending)
Solicitation	Marketed over Internet, TV, social media , etc., via advertisements or direct marketing	Marketed over Internet, TV, social media, etc. However, primary solicitation must be via registered portal; all other means "restricted"
Elegible Issuers	Both SEC- registered and private companies companies	Non-SEC registered companies only
Elegible Investors	Accredited investors only	Anyone eligible if they demonstrate understanding of investment. Dollar amount limited.
Determining Investor Eligibility	Various "verification" methods permitted	TBD
Offering Size Limit	No dollar limit	$1 million (some issues still TBD)
Intermediaries	Not required; any intermediaries used must be registered broker-dealers or exempt	Intermediaries are compulsory; funding portals or broker-dealers
Disclosure	Driven by market demands and liability concerns	Audited statements, disclosures mandated by law. Additional disclosure likely. TBD
Filing Requirements	Prior filing of Form D, amendment post-closing, informal submission of solicitation materials to SEC	SEC filing required; form TBD

*Derived from a table created by Sarah Hanks and originally published at www.crowdcheck.com, 2013.

FIGURE 3.4: *Regulatory overview of Rule 506 and likely legal framework for crowdfunding*

- Do references check out? Good fundraising partners live off their investor relationships and their reputation as a good and fair company. References should be relevant, in context, and current.
- What is the culture of the entity? Hopefully the prospective partner can speak positively of his or her own firm's culture and give you a sense of the firm's values and commitment to clients.
- What is their method of conducting deals? How do they interact with your prospective investors? There is no clear right answer, but this question is especially important to ask.
- Do you trust them? Basic trust is essential—if you do not have trust, you have nothing. Listen to your gut.
- Many investors want direct contact—particularly for early stage investments—and do not want (or appreciate) a middleman. What will your fundraising partner do if an investor voices that preference? The best answer is that they won't get in the way of a deal, and will continue to make themselves valuable.
- If you are interviewing a third-party marketer, ask them if they use a mass-canvassing approach. Good third-party marketers are focused on targeting investors specifically. If their approach involves spamming, they are not worth your time.

Ideal fundraising partners understand investors' needs and desires. They employ a rational, systematic approach to canvassing for an investor fit. This means doing lots of tedious research. Your partner should understand the value of fit, and be able to prove how they plan to match investors with you.

If you have decided that the best way for you to raise money is via a fundraising partner, be sure to get sound advice and do your research. Discussions with other successful entrepreneurs in the life science space, legal experts, and respected industry players will help lead you in the right direction.

CHAPTER 4

Categories of
Life Science Investors

The investor landscape within the life sciences has undergone significant change in recent times. There is a broad range of investors with varying appetites and approaches to allocations within the life science space, and in order to fully understand exactly why this is the case, it is critical to take a look at private investment trends before and after the 2008 recession (see Figure 4.1).[6]

Historically, venture capitalists (VCs) dominated investment in life sciences. There were a large number of sophisticated funds consistently allocating to emerging life science companies, from early to late stages of development. There was also an understanding among these venture capitalists that the life sciences constitutes a complex investment arena that requires a long-term orientation and a sophisticated understanding of the science involved, the regulatory risks, and the full process of innovation, from discovery to distribution.

---

[6] For more detailed information on changes to the categories of life science investors, see "The View Beyond Venture Capital" by Dennis Ford and Barbara Nelsen, published in *Nature* magazine on January 8, 2014, which appears in its entirety in the Addendum of this book.

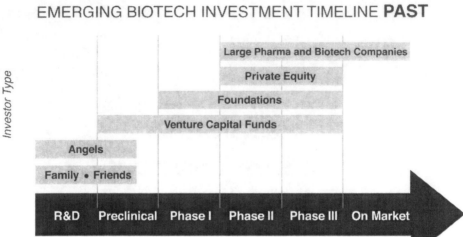

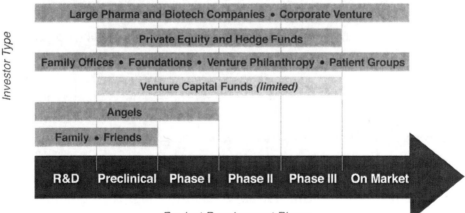

FIGURE 4.1: *The shift within the life science investor landscape and the entities filling the venture capital (VC) gap*

This thoughtful investment approach and complex understanding of the life science arena produced some big-time successes in the form of initial public offerings (IPOs) and mergers and acquisitions. Consequently, a few decades ago, many opportunistic VC funds without a historical interest in the space were lured by the promise of outsized returns and a booming IPO market. By the time of the economic downturn of 2008, which affected the entire global marketplace, there was a lot of opportunistic capital allocated in a very high-risk asset class. As a result, these new life science VC funds became an underperforming asset class with poor returns, protracted exit timelines, and a very disappointed investor base. So what happened next?

The first thing to occur was that many investors that were once limited partners in VC funds began to withdraw their capital and debate whether to make these high-risk, high-return investments themselves. This is most prominently reflected by the rise in the number of family offices investing directly in the life science arena. This, in turn, caused a distinct thinning of the early stage life science VC funds, which consolidated into only a few dozen that continued to make allocations on a reliable basis, albeit with a focus toward mid- to late-stage life science companies. A void was left in the early stage life science investor space, leaving a lot of great technology underfunded.

However, at the same time, a plethora of new investors began to emerge alongside the family offices going direct. These included syndicated angel groups, those participating in the nascent crowdfunding phenomenon (which has received lots of hype but has not proven its worth to the life sciences at the time of this book's publication), mid-level private equity firms, big pharma and corporate VC, foundations, endowments, pension funds, and venture philanthropy or patient groups, as well as hybrids of all of the above.

This chapter seeks to elucidate the new landscape of private investments in the life science space (see Figure 4.1), the way in which a life science CEO should think of both the traditional and new investor categories, and some key points on how to approach these entities. The primary business of Life Science Nation (LSN) is to conduct private investor research in the life science space. LSN tracks 10 categories of active investors around the globe on an ongoing basis in the form of in-depth investor interviews. This gives LSN a forward-looking picture of investor intent for approximately 5,000 investors currently allocating in the space.[7] Figure 4.2 shows a high-level overview of the early stage investor space for therapeutics.

The chart represents approximately 2,500 life science investors that LSN has tracked to date that are interested in early stage investment in therapeutics and devices; there are also 2,500 interested in later-stage clinical assets or on-the-market products and services. We examine the state of these categories on a high level to help you, as a fundraising executive, map a route to market.

Friends and Family

Although friends, family members, and high–net-worth individuals are important investors in the life science food chain, LSN does not cover these types of investors. LSN spends most of its research efforts going after "institutional" investors; the investors in this group typically manage assets ranging in value from $100 million to over $1 billion.

However, friends and family are often a primary source of capital during the early formation of an emerging life science company. These investors constitute those with whom you have personal relationships who have the ability to support the first steps toward commercializing your product. As such, they are worth mentioning briefly.

These are potential investors who might be willing to bet on your ability and take a risk on your success. They represent an opportunity for your company to make its first efforts at fundraising. Every situation is differ-

---

[7]This number is accurate as of March 2014, but it is growing. We are constantly adding to the LSN database; the current rate is between 25 and 35 new investors per week.

EARLY STAGE LIFE SCIENCE INVESTORS*

	Medical Technology	Therapeutics & Diagnostics
Angel Group	86	83
Corporate Venture Capital	39	50
Foundations & Philanthropic	49	108
Family Offices & Private Wealth	17	59
Government Organizations	47	77
Hedge Funds	5	12
Institutional Alternative Investors (Pensions, Endowments)	25	54
Large Pharma & Biotech	7	46
Private Equity	286	386
Venture Capital	521	572
Total	1,082	1,447

*This reflects the landscape of investors with a declared interest in early stage (seed or venture) investments in discovery-phase I biotech assets or prototype-clinical stage medical.

FIGURE 4.2: *An overview of the new early stage investor landscape. Source: LSN Investor Database, 2014*

ent, but taking money from family and close friends is the way many entrepreneurs get off the ground. LSN is focused on the investor landscape past this point—when you launch your first institutional-style fundraising round. Let's go through the categories of the investors you'll encounter on this level.

Angel Syndicates

Angel syndicates are essentially groups of high-net-worth individuals with an interest in direct private investment who have affiliated themselves in order to leverage their collective expertise for due diligence purposes and to increase the amount of capital they can deploy, adding weight to their placements. Angel groups are often among the earliest investors in an emerging life science company (typically investing between $250,000 and $2 million), and they bring with them some significant advantages and disadvantages. On the upside, they have an appetite for risk and are undeterred by the challenges that emerging companies face. Early stage investments are what these folks focus on. However, angel syndicates are loose affiliations of individuals, which can make the processes of negotiation and investor relationship management seem like exercises in herding cats. Also, due to the regional nature of most angel groups, an emerging company is often restricted geographically in terms of which angels are a fit.

LSN tracks about 100 active angel groups and syndicates investing in biotech and medtech companies around the world. LSN has found that roughly 80% of these groups are interested in life science assets that are in a preclinical stage (such as therapeutics) or a prototype stage (such as devices). Now let's get into how to approach this category.

Understanding what angels are looking for in companies—and how to set yourself apart from the crowd—can make or break your campaign. Angels, like other early stage investors, have been burned by bad returns over the past decade, and those that remain have a tight grip on their capital. In order to loosen that grip, your pitch must immediately catch the investors' attention by engaging them—not drowning them in slides of text and data. Here are some general guidelines to follow:

- **Tell your story.** Who are you? Why did you start this company? How did the management team first get together? Where did the initial idea come from? These questions, which can be answered within the first few minutes of a presentation, are ones that angels can relate to, regardless of their understanding of the science and technology that is driving the company. When investors have a foundational understanding of the roots of your organization, they get a better feel for the drivers of the company as a whole and can more easily put their trust in you.

- **Address the market.** Oftentimes, early stage entrepreneurs are caught up in the "cool factor" of their technologies and haven't given enough thought to the actual marketplace. Discuss the medical need your product is addressing and what treatment options are currently available for it. Here you have the opportunity to capture the investors' attention by showing them the potential revenue your firm may realize if your product reaches the market.

- **Hit them with the technology.** This is the section of the presentation that too often reminds investors of an academic chemistry lecture and prompts them to check out within minutes. When addressing how your device functions or the pathways your therapeutic is targeting, you need to show enthusiasm and passion. Having high energy and excitement when explaining the technology shows that you yourself believe in the product and that what you are working on is innovative and investment-worthy. (It will also keep investors awake.)

- **Know what you want.** Instead of only communicating how much capital you need to get to clinical trials, you should have diagrams in your presentation highlighting exactly how much of the requested funding is going to be spent on the various activities your company must perform.

Essentially, you need to make your appeal to angels as understandable, logical, and personable as possible, because at the end of the day, they're going to be investing in you and your management team as much as your technology.

Venture Capital

As already discussed extensively, VC has consolidated substantially in recent history, and fewer funds remain reliably active at the early stage. LSN tracks less than 1,000 early stage VCs—and a small subset of these firms represent the majority of financings today. These are the large, big-name funds that are in every life science entrepreneur's vocabulary. They are the survivors of the post-recession fallout, and for good reason. They are highly sophisticated, have a sound understanding of the marketplace, and employ top-tier operations talent.

However, if you are an entrepreneur courting these investors, it will benefit you to be wary. The remaining active VC funds know that they have an advantage in that they are the first investors in every entrepreneur's mind, meaning they have the pick of the litter among early stage companies who are all jockeying for the same capital. This gives them the luxury of offering less-than-stellar terms to entrepreneurs when it comes to valuations and capital structures, and oftentimes they can leave a CEO in a tough position. Venture capitalists can be viable partners, but it is critical that an entrepreneur makes sure that visions are aligned, that the valuation and the terms are fair, and that too much equity and control isn't surrendered too early in the process.

Family Offices

Family offices are among the most stealthy investor groups in the life science space, and many of the entrepreneurs with whom my company works are initially unfamiliar with this category. Family offices basically act as personal CFOs for ultra-high-net-worth families and individuals—their scope includes generational wealth management, philanthropic donations, legal issues, and management of tangible assets. Each family office is unique in that its services are a function of the demands, skills, and financial requirements of the families, family, or individual whose money they manage.

These organizations exist primarily in two basic forms: single family offices (SFOs) and multi-family offices (MFOs) (see Figure 4.3). SFOs,

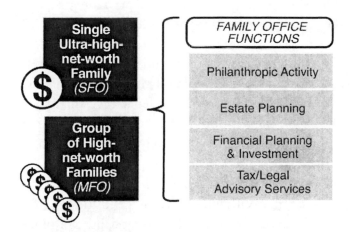

FIGURE 4.3: *Visualizing the family office*

as the name suggests, manage the finances for a single family or individual. LSN tracks SFOs with a net worth of at least $100 million, and some have over $1 billion. The average family office manages approximately $600 million. MFOs, which recently have been gaining popularity, cater to the needs of multiple families with a minimum net worth of around $20 million and an average of about $50 million. However, in aggregate, MFOs and SFOs are dealing with comparable asset pools. This allows families with lower net worth to collectively leverage the same advantages that an SFO provides.

The amount of capital held by family offices has been growing recently, as more traditional wealth managers (following the market demand for complete personalized financial management) are offering more holistic services, transforming their business models to become MFOs. Another reason for the increase in family office capital has been the recent tendency for MFOs to lower their asset requirements. Industry experts estimate that there are currently over 4,000 family offices in the United States alone, with well over $1 trillion in combined assets under management, making them a very significant source of private capital.

Historically, family offices have allocated a portion of their capital to alternative assets, such as VC funds, hedge funds, and private equity funds. Many family offices involved in the life science direct investment trend are utilizing the skills and knowledge of the particular sector that made the family its fortune to identify strong investment opportunities, where they also have the ability to add value beyond capital. This authority, combined with the fact that many family offices see life science investment as an opportunity to participate in the development of therapy for an ailment prevalent in the family, is making them an incredibly powerful presence in the life science investment space.

What's more, as long as family offices have been in existence, the majority (over 50% globally, and an even higher percentage in the U.S.) have maintained a portion of their clients' capital for the purpose of philanthropic allocations. Recently, there has been a trend for philanthropy to be less of a donation and more of an investment, with a focus on a measurable, positive social impact on society as a gauge of the ROI (return on investment). With this mind-set, family offices are investing directly into industries such as the life sciences, where a scientific breakthrough could have massive, lasting positive impact on a global scale. Family offices looking for an impact with their investments do not have the same standards for ROI as traditional investment firms, who are under immense pressure to generate consistent returns by shareholders, and are therefore offering better terms with less stringent restrictions on time-to-exit than traditional private investors.

LSN has identified close to 1,000 family offices globally that constitute a potential investor base for life science entrepreneurs. Approximately 400 of these have established activity within the life sciences or are actively seeking investment opportunities to move science forward via direct investment.

Hedge Funds

There is a broad range of hedge fund types, which could constitute their own book, but an easy way to think of them is as managed portfolios of stocks, bonds, derivatives, commodities, or any other such set of assets. Hedge funds are traditionally thought of as players active only in public markets. However, as fund managers have come under increased pressure to generate outsized returns on behalf of their investors, many managers have turned to more esoteric strategies and have gotten more creative when it comes to making allocations. For example, some hedge funds incorporate a PIPE (Private Investment in Public Equity) strategy, which allows them to make a private placement into a publicly traded company (typically at a discount and in exchange for some other additional benefits).

Others have employed a special situations strategy, which takes advantage of opportunities that are out of the public equity and into the private investment arena. This can either be in the form of one-off "side pocket" investments on an opportunistic basis or an integrated piece of an investment strategy. LSN has identified over 80 hedge funds that have begun to make this sort of "crossover investment" in the life science arena.

Mid-Level Private Equity

Private equity (PE) is also challenging the historical map—PE is traditionally thought of as the capital used in the restructuring of large, post-revenue companies. However, this is changing—especially in the life science space. Biotech and medtech opportunities have a high potential for returns, and PE firms have a higher tolerance for the long timeline to commercialization. Many firms have therefore begun implementing strategies to aggregate assets and shepherd them through the pipeline. This portfolio of assets can then be passed to a large strategic partner as a one-stop solution to a pipeline gap, where a full portfolio of drugs is worth more than the sum of its parts. LSN tracks about 1,700 PE funds investing in the life sciences around the world and roughly 400 that are active in emerging biotech and medtech companies.

Big Pharma and Big Biotech

Increasingly, over the past few years, large pharmaceutical and biotech companies have been slashing basic in-house R&D budgets at a fast clip. Coming at a time when the industry is performing remarkably well and basic R&D is more critical than ever, this trend might confuse observers. However, what many do not recognize is that the primary motivation for this trend is not only to cut costs (though it is saving considerable money for many firms). Rather, it is reflective of a novel means by which the R&D pipeline is being approached from the ground up, reflecting major changes in the industry over the past decade. In the past, pipeline gaps were filled with the intent of maintaining market share, and in order for a biotech company to be a fit, their product needed to be relatively far down the pipeline. Now all of that is changing.

The reason for this has been a massive paradigm shift in the collective "big pharma" psyche. The nature of the marketplace has changed in that the best researchers with the best ideas are no longer seeking out positions within big pharma but instead are starting their own companies, largely due to the fact that CROs and other outsourcing partners in the space have made it possible to do groundbreaking research with minimal investment in infrastructure. Some might see this as a problem, as big pharma seems to be starved for innovation and desperately needs to refill dry pipelines. However, this isn't necessarily bad news—the opportunity for big pharma to selectively buy into independently developed projects on a global basis allows for a geared ROI on the R&D budget and introduces an enormous amount of fresh capital to the marketplace at the early stage.

Traditionally, big pharma wasn't even on an emerging biotech company's radar screen until a product was entering late-stage clinical trials and required a strategic partner to enable it to enter the marketplace. Additionally, the big pharma and biotech firms' search and evaluation teams tended to focus their energy on discovering opportunities to plug *existing* pipeline gaps closer to market and not on early stage assets that could form the basis of the forward-looking R&D pipeline. This is changing rapidly and the implications are massive; big pharma is increasingly focusing efforts on investing in small and emerging biotech firms. LSN tracks close to 100 of these entities around the world.

The majority of corporate investments are structured in four forms: direct investments from the parent company, wholly owned subsidiaries, independent organizations with dedicated funds, and limited partners in other funds. Understanding the type of corporate investment a company is interested in making will be critical in determining your ability to catch their interest.

Corporate Venture Capital

Corporate venture capital (CVC) is a strategy that has been adopted by a number of large corporations to enable them to have a hand in emerging technologies that are either directly or indirectly aligned with their primary business. CVC funds are essentially VC funds backed by the capital of a primary corporation. LSN tracks approximately 100 corporate venture capitalists with a declared life science interest.

CVC funding is particularly beneficial for new ventures in the life sciences that operate in uncertain environments, because this funding often comes with specialized assets and knowledge. Over one-third of active corporate venture capitalists that LSN tracks are healthcare focused. Additionally, studies have shown that financing rounds with CVC involved tend to be significantly higher than non-CVC funded rounds. The innovation output of CVC-funded companies is also higher, as measured by the number of their publications and patents.

Recently, corporate venture capitalists have actually started co-investing in rounds with each other. At first, this might appear to make little sense, as the parent companies are directly competing for the same technologies. However, as the CVC firms have become more familiar with each other, they have begun to understand how each structures their deals and are becoming more comfortable sharing the table with another big name player. The shift toward independently operating venture funds is big pharma's method of keeping the innovation pipeline flowing in response to the decline of truly early stage in-house R&D funding. This is good news for early stage ventures and should be carefully considered when planning a fundraising strategy.

Pensions and Endowments

Pensions and endowments are typically highly sophisticated institutional investors backed by very large asset pools. Increasingly, these large institutional investors with the flexibility to be somewhat opportunistic in their investment mandates have begun making direct placements into life science companies. LSN tracks close to 100 pensions and endowments with an active interest in direct investment in the life sciences.

When dealing with these entities, it is critical to ensure that your company's risk profile is explained as clearly as possible. Though these investments are typically made outside of the chartered investment mandate, most of these groups will still maintain a high degree of risk scrutiny while evaluating your proposition. Pensions are usually interested in late-stage companies, but some are willing to look at pre-revenue companies and even companies that have preclinical assets.

In the endowments space, investors are also starting to make direct investments. Endowments are oftentimes heavily invested in the PE space, as they have longer-term investment horizons than other investors. They are thus comfortable with the lengthy lock-up periods that many direct investment opportunities stipulate. Endowments in the life sciences are certainly beginning to go direct, but on a smaller scale when compared with pension funds. Endowments are particularly interested in investing in companies that are harnessing technologies that were spun out of their own institution, but are increasingly investing in companies that are developing technologies from outside universities as well.

Pensions and endowments tend to be guided by highly sophisticated process and procedure, so making the correct first impression with them is vital. Clarity, transparency, and a willingness to collaborate with resources made available by the investor (especially in the case of university endowments) are extremely helpful assets. A good starting point is to find a navigator who can explain the desired format for submission of an investment proposal, specific requirements in terms of data, and any other conditions that must be met.

Foundations, Venture Philanthropy, and Patient Groups

Foundations have been a fixture of the life science space for a long time, but historically they were primarily grant-writing organizations. However, recently they have joined the ranks of venture philanthropists and patient groups to comprise some of the most interesting equity investor categories to emerge in recent history. LSN tracks approximately 250 of these entities around the world. Though they target different diseases in different ways, they all share a unified mission—to help researchers move the science along in a particular area.

Foundations and venture philanthropy groups have significant overlap in that they are using an equity investment model that is focused on driving commercialization to push a philanthropic agenda. It has become evident that for a therapy to reach the market, philanthropic organizations need to have skin in the game and an incentive to keep moving the science forward. This model is rapidly gaining momentum and has the dual advantages of making foundations focus on a long-term relationship with funded companies as well as providing a source of returns that scales with the organization over time to enhance impact.

A patient group is a collection of individuals afflicted by a disease who come together and mobilize to find a cure for their particular affliction. In the past, patient groups oftentimes partnered with foundations (or venture philanthropists) in order to make an investment. One example of this was the Cystic Fibrosis Foundation partnering with a number of patient groups and Aurora BioScience. Now, however, the industry is seeing more and more of these patient groups mobilizing other groups in order to make a strategic investment to more directly improve patient outcomes.

Patient groups are taking an innovative approach to investing in the life science space. To push research along in a certain area, patient groups will often take a strategic approach and attempt to bring many parties together, such as scientists who are researching different elements of the disease— usually the best and most well-known scientists in the space to ensure legitimacy—in order to foster a collaborative environment. Patient groups then establish their clinical network, which is a network of patients that can be utilized for clinical trials for companies in which they invest (made up of members of the patient group who are afflicted by the disease). The final step for these patient groups is to bring biotech and big pharma companies into the picture; these companies help the scientists to commercialize their research.

Patient groups are also dynamic because they almost create an ecosystem within their particular disease focus. Generally patient groups are huge advocates of sharing as much information as possible, and they help researchers, even those outside of their network, to gain access to research and data more quickly and easily than they would otherwise. Patient groups also help patients to educate themselves and allow them to see the various treatment options that are available to them that may not yet be FDA approved. Thus it is expected that patient groups will start to become major players in the life science investment space.

Venture philanthropists, foundations, and patient groups are eager to meet their goal of accelerating the development of treatments and cures for the world's most challenging diseases. One group actively moving this agenda forward is FasterCures, a center of the Milken Institute. This organization's mission is to facilitate a collective alliance among venture philanthropy groups, patient advocacy groups, foundations, family offices, regulatory authorities, and big pharma companies. Their TRAIN group (The Research Acceleration and Innovation Network) is made up of approximately 75 active philanthropic entities that are focused on moving science into the hands of patients for a broad range of diseases. These organizations provide over $600 million in medical research capital annually. About half of the TRAIN group has supported at least one clinical trial, more than half incorporate advocacy efforts into their work in fighting disease, and nearly 9 out of 10 TRAIN entities partner with biotechnology and pharmaceutical companies.

There is a high degree of direct involvement with these groups; these are hands-on investors. They are more open than many other investors, and therefore flexible deal terms with multi-year allocation timelines can be negotiated. They know how to get things done, so expect milestones and carefully scrutinized metrics, along with action plans and organizational input.

These entities provide funding for scientists and young life science companies in order to move along the development of therapies for certain diseases. Unlike traditional philanthropic organizations, they expect the companies and individuals they invest in to achieve certain preset goals and focus on accountability. They aren't only funding basic research; they are helping to drive products to patients as quickly and efficiently as possible.

These investors are becoming increasingly important, especially due to the inability of many scientists to translate discoveries into compelling market opportunities and because of impending cuts in the NIH budget, which could cripple future therapy development. Currently, venture philanthropy only represents less than 3% of the spending on medical R&D in the U.S., but this figure is expected to rise as the need for funding from scientists and early stage biotech firms continues to grow.

Crowdfunding

Crowdfunding (as already mentioned in Chapters 2 and 3) is a paradigm shift. It bears mentioning here since, in theory, it represents a new category of investors: the general public. However, the ante required to get into the game is one of the most important elements to question. Some sites are demanding fees or a portion of the capital raised, which can be 5% to 20%—that's a pretty steep price of admission for a virtual company profile and a three-minute video. The first crowdfunding portals and their associated business models are varied in their policies, so do your own research. The mantra used by the entrepreneurs who run these portals is essentially as follows: *the risk to the investor is low because the investment dollar amount is low, and the people will decide what makes its way into the market.*

Translating this into iterative, experiment-based life science technologies may be tricky, as the general public isn't necessarily going to fully understand the subtleties of therapeutic biomarkers, mechanisms of action, or physics-based, next-gen medical devices. Therefore, the obvious candidates for this kind of funding are healthcare IT companies and easily comprehendible medical devices; if start-ups in therapeutic technologies are to pursue crowdfunding, then they must ensure that their product and technology is framed in terms that are easily understood by a layperson.

Keeping it simple and using crowdfunding as a tactic for part of the strategy for early stage capital fundraising may be fine. However, it won't be *the* full-blown solution to the industry's capital needs.

Summary

As you can see, the fundraising landscape for early stage life science companies reflects a broad range of investors with different priorities, investment interests, and levels of activity. Recent years have brought many changes to the life science investment arena; for example, the differences between VC, PE, and hedge funds are starting to blur, and all three of these entities have established themselves as having constituents that are investing in early stage life science companies. This is good news, because these players have large capital reserves and can bring a significant amount of cash back into the early stage marketplace.

Though transformations such as these have already altered the playing field, the landscape has likely not completed its shift—more change is yet to come. This demands that life science executives, now more than ever, do their homework as to which investor categories represent a potential fit over the full life of the company. Only after this road map has been established will you be ready to begin formulating an outbound fundraising strategy to raise capital.

CHAPTER 5

Knowing Who and What You Are, and Where You Fit

"Pivoting" is a word that's thrown around a lot by the business press—most often in the software space, where it's used to refer to the practice of rapidly updating a new product in response to customer feedback. This practice has given rise to an entire school of thought on how to make a start-up company succeed. These days, defining who you are, what exactly you are offering, and where you fit in the marketplace and pitching your product to potential investors is not a linear process. Instead, outside feedback is critical in helping you to pivot your message and even sometimes your identity so that the process of reaching the marketplace becomes a feedback loop.

If you're seeking to understand more about entrepreneurship in the life science arena, you can quickly become immersed in the dialogue that is out there on the Internet, ranging from the rich and provocative commentary found on steveblank.com to Life Science Nation (LSN) weekly newsletter content to articles in the Harvard and Stanford business publications. In this chapter, I will try to distill some of that commentary and provide some practical input on the process of creating your identity by pivoting in response to outside feedback.

There is one thing you have to understand before you get started: fundraising is as complex and difficult a process as science itself, and just as with experiments in the lab, the success-to-failure ratio is high. Here is a very general rule of thumb: if you contact 200 to 300 investors that are generally a decent fit and then perform a diligent follow-up, you may create a dialogue with 40 to 60 of them. In the end, 8 to 12 investors may build a relationship with you, and 1 or 2 may actually allocate to you. It will never be easy. You're probably not going to get a deal on the first phone call, or even at the first meeting, so you shouldn't make that your goal. LSN research has found that with a strong global target list (GTL), outbound fundraisers may be able to set up meetings with up to 20% of the investors they contact—a hit rate that any sales executive would envy—but getting to the table is only the first step on the path to receiving investment. However, what every meeting offers you is an opportunity to test the effectiveness of your message before a live audience.

Given how many years of development it takes to get a life science product into the marketplace, investors offer your first real-world testing opportunity. Many of them will be more experienced than you are regarding your market segment, regulatory issues, or the ins and outs of reimbursement; more than that, as you've come to them for money, they will have to put themselves in the role of a customer in your market and make a cold, hard assessment of the potential value of your product. The investor therefore provides you with a chance at getting valuable customer feedback that in other industries serves as fuel for pivoting.

If you do reach a deal from the first meeting, that's wonderful—but it should be regarded as a happy accident. It's far more likely that you'll be speaking to a dozen or more potential investors before you find someone who wants to back you. But each time you deliver your pitch to an investor, you're engaging in a valuable learning opportunity. Above all, pivoting is the art of not wasting those opportunities.

You Can't Adapt the Message Without a Real Audience

The truth is that you can't learn how effective your message is until you go out there and deliver it to as many investors as possible. Financial advisors and business consultants can give you valuable input, but the true assessment comes from those asked to stake real money on your success.

Agonizing over every detail of your messaging before going out there to talk to potential investors is a waste of your time. Instead, you need to accept that you don't have all the information yet; you need to book some meetings with investors, put on the best presentation you can, and listen carefully to the responses you receive.

Tailor your pitch for each type of investor and tweak the presentation after each meeting to incorporate what you just learned. So, for example, if you've given your tailored presentation to an angel investor with experience in the medical industry and the investor wasn't wowed, ask why not! Don't be shy, and don't chalk it up to an off day or a clumsy handshake. You have to accept that the investor made a rational decision not to back you. Ask what you're lacking, substantively, that might have changed that decision. Be prepared to accept that you're making mistakes, and then fix those mistakes.

Adapting your message might be as simple as tailoring your presentation better. Did the investor tell you that your product was too scientifically complex to risk money on? That's probably a signal that you need message adaptation; you were speaking in a language that the investor didn't understand, when instead you should have been connecting on his or her own level by discussing how soon the product could reach market or how your product is going to out-compete rival solutions. Or perhaps the investor will tell you that you seem overconfident regarding the opportunity and are failing to consider the obstacles x, y, and z that the investor is already aware of due to past experience. You can then add your responses to these challenges to your messaging and turn this weakness into a strength.

Such cosmetic changes are relatively easy to contemplate. But if you're repeatedly encountering poor results even after you've received plenty of feedback and updated your messaging, you may need to consider the need for a more serious pivot to your company's direction.

Major changes of direction are more common in the life sciences than you might think. Due to the complexity of human biology, it's rare for any product to affect only one working part of the whole body. You are probably aware of multiple potential applications for your product; perhaps one of the avenues you didn't originally consider would be an easier regulatory market, a larger opportunity, or less competition than you've encountered on your current path. We have all heard the stories of developing for x and solving problem y. For example, a cardiac researcher developed a novel drug delivery device to treat myocardial infarction; during the development process, he realized that the best market opportunity for the product was in treating Achilles tendon injuries! These situations are not as uncommon as you may think.

There's no shortage of examples of life science companies that were forced to deviate from their original plan to reach market. You might be developing a drug discovery platform but then find that there's more potential in developing the molecules or biologics that you identify than in selling the platform itself. Or you might be planning to market your diagnostic device directly to physicians and then realize you could get more market share by selling to hospitals instead. Healthcare is what's called a multi-sided market; regulators, large pharma companies, hospitals, care providers, HMOs, and patients are all involved in the adoption of your product and in the eventual generation of revenue, and you may very well need to rethink your approach to any one of these market segments.

You should also bear in mind that the investor is betting on the strength of not only the product but also the management team. Is your team well-rounded? Maybe the investor expressed worries about your lack of industry experience; in that case, you can consider finding an industry veteran to serve as your team's advisor.

Examine Your Business Model

According to one well-known guide, *Business Model Generation* by Alexander Osterwalder, a business model comprises nine components:

- Value proposition—the product that you're developing and its potential value to an investor
- Customer segments—selected from within the multi-sided health-care market
- Channels—the distribution methods through which the product will reach the customers

- Customer relationships—how you find customers and keep them
- Key partners—may include material suppliers, CROs, and academic facilities, and will certainly include your investors
- Key activities—include clinical trials and regulatory filings
- Key resources—often include intellectual property and key research facilities and collaborators
- Costs—which define the length of your runway
- Revenue streams—in which reimbursement is a vital consideration

For a start-up in any industry, the initial business model, no matter how clear and well conceptualized, is in fact only a rough sketch—you don't yet *know* if your model going to work, and you have to accept that parts of it might not survive your company's first encounters with the real world. For example, you might have realized by reading this book that you need to change your model of how to build relationships with investors. That's a pivot to your model in itself. But if your search for funds is getting you nowhere, it's worth considering every part of the business model. Are you failing to explain part of the model to investors, or does the model itself need an overhaul? In order to have a positive effect, change has to be substantial and meaningful. If you pivot as you move along, you can incorporate what you have learned.

Know Your Space

When you deliver your pitch to investors, many of them will be paying close attention to how much awareness you have of the market for your product. Negotiating the existing marketplace is a vastly complex endeavor, and entrepreneurs who are new to the industry may have a lot to learn in this regard.

Investors, particularly generalist fund managers who might be more accustomed to investing in other areas of technology, will want you to show a good grasp of "customer-market fit." You have to know who your patients are, who's providing them with medical care, what products they're using at the present, and how the current solution generates revenue (which may be a reimbursement quagmire). You have to show how your product will represent a better solution for these patients and their care providers than what they have at present. You have to know the size of this market and how much revenue your product is capable of generating. Additionally, you have to be aware of the regulatory paths for products like yours and what you'll have to do to get the regulator's approval.

It's been proven that the best technology in the world won't save you if you don't understand the market. Highly effective new drugs and diagnostics have been driven out of the marketplace because their developers failed to solve the reimbursement problem. Innovative medical devices have failed because the developers didn't account for competition; it can be hard to build market share for a new type of catheter, for example, because hospitals have so many existing catheters to choose from.

It's been said that the sales process is first about listening to customers and understanding what they need and then demonstrating that your product will serve that need. Investors will need to be shown that you're engaging with that process even in the early stages of development and are aware of all the market risks you're asking them to face alongside you.

On the upside, learning about your market isn't going to cost your company a great deal, and in healthcare, there are often a wealth of resources to aid you. Charitable foundations can be very useful partners for an emerging company; many offer small grants or venture philanthropy financing to companies performing early stage research in their disease area of concern, but these groups are more than just investors. They're also experts on both the science and the industry of their indication, and many offer access to a patient registry for use in clinical trials. Building a relationship with a foundation can therefore be of huge benefit to you, even if they're not able to offer funding to your company.

Embrace Chaos

This process of finding the right message and the right business model might seem chaotic. In a sense, it's *meant* to be chaotic. Adopting a pivot mentality means accepting that you don't know everything about your product's journey to the marketplace and being prepared to adapt as you go. For a start-up, your business plan should always be a work in progress.

Indeed, in this book we've given you a road map of the transformed life science investor landscape, but this too is a work in progress. Undoubtedly this landscape will continue to change in the future, and your fundraising campaigns will have to keep up with new investor trends. As you undertake further fundraising rounds, you'll be constantly learning about new investors in the life science space.

And in addition to learning from chaos and difficulties, you can also learn from your successes and serendipity. If you get a positive response from an investor, you should always ask to be put in touch with their network of co-investors, those who have invested alongside them in companies like yours in the past. Each of those investors may provide you with further opportunities to adapt.

It's Never Too Early

Scientists often tell us that they don't want to leave the lab just yet. They need to do more research before starting a fundraising campaign; they need to finalize their development plan and get every detail right in order to make the most compelling pitch to investors that those investors have ever heard. Or perhaps they need to get more personal referrals to investors from their professional network before they're willing to pick up the phone.

This attitude will only hold you back. It's a form of perfectionism, which is fear based and leads to an assumption that outside feedback, whether positive or negative, is the final judgment of a start-up's worth, rather than an instrumental tool to be utilized in creating a successful company. It won't serve you in the real world.

You have to accept that fundraising and relationship building are slow processes. It normally takes 9 to 12 months or more to complete a financing round; many companies have failed simply because the scientists kept the company holed up in the lab until they ran out of runway, not realizing how long it would take to raise the funds necessary to complete their research. It's never too soon to start building your investor network.

You should think ahead of time. Perhaps you're raising money to cover a phase I trial and you've made a call to a private equity firm, only to find out that while they are very interested in your technology, they don't want to invest until you've finished phase II. Keep them in the loop! Inform them of your research successes as they occur, and when you've reached a stage where you match their criteria, maybe they'll want to lead your next financing round. By keeping up a relationship, you'll actually increase your chances of this happening, since people in general are always more inclined to contribute to individuals and companies they "know."

And it's never too early to learn about your market and about who's presently investing there. Finding those investors who are a good fit for your company will help you far more than getting referrals to investors who may not be interested in your technology at all.

Pivoting Doesn't Mean Throwing Your Work Away

So you've been talking to investors for a few weeks, and maybe you've realized that part of your original vision has to change. Perhaps you've learned that your regulation pathway is onerous and now you're planning to apply for a CE mark rather than FDA approval. Or you've discovered that there's a suitable indication area for your product that provides a stronger market opportunity than the one you were originally pursuing. This can be particularly tough for a researcher who has focused his or her entire career on a particular indication; pivoting to target a new one might feel like abandoning your dreams.

It's important to remember that you're not abandoning your prior work, merely rethinking it. That original opportunity you looked into hasn't gone *away*; it's just not the best path to market. Everything you've learned about your original vision still has value, and changing your model doesn't detract from that. Investors will indeed be glad to know that there are several potential market opportunities for your product and that you have an avenue to create extra value for them down the line by engaging with multiple markets.

You can't be too attached to your original plan. One thing we hear a lot from investors is that they want to back savvy entrepreneurs who display the industry know-how needed to get their product to market, not hyperfocused lab researchers who may have unlocked an amazing discovery but don't seem to have a realistic idea of the discovery's real-world value or path to market. The best life science entrepreneurs work in a truly inter-disciplinary fashion; they have an awareness of their product's range of potential applications along with the business smarts to make it happen. Your new knowledge and ideas will add to your existing knowledge and ideas, not displace them, and now you'll find you have all the resources required to create a strong message for your company.

Parsing Technology

One way of parsing the life science landscape is on the basis of technology. Life science start-ups can be divided into three broad categories: those that offer disruptive technology, those focusing on significant breakthroughs or "leapfrog" technology, and those offering iterative technology (see Figure 5.1). Each category comes with its own benefits and shortcomings and has the capacity to attract the right investors. However, there is a hierarchy when it comes to investor interest, so you'll need to understand where your company's products fit on this scale in order to position yourself best and find the right investor audience for your company.

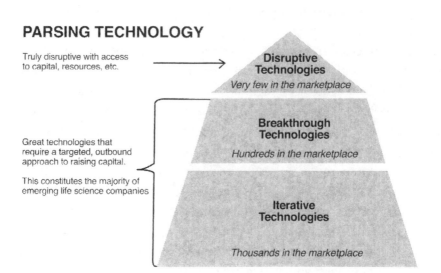

FIGURE 5.1: *Understanding the technology landscape in the life sciences*

Life science companies with "disruptive" technologies have the potential to change the world in a big way. The word "disruptive" is often overused in the life science industry, so I'd like to take a moment to explain exactly what it means. Disruptive technologies are those that literally disrupt the industry by driving an advancement that completely changes the marketplace within one or several indications. This is the rare technology that is groundbreaking on a huge scale; a cure for diabetes or an AIDS vaccine would be examples of these kinds of developments. These companies represent billion dollar opportunities and are typically quickly identified and shepherded to the top-tier venture capitalists. There are very few start-ups who fall into this category.

The companies with "breakthrough" technology represent significant solutions for major medical needs. These can be viewed as "leapfrog technologies" that change treatment paradigms or improve outcomes in a big way. These are not necessarily disruptive, but they are undoubtedly valuable innovations that impact patients substantially. These breakthrough companies might number in the hundreds, and they are tasked with marketing themselves to the right investors, because the shrinking venture capital (VC) population isn't necessarily accessible to them and may not be the best fit for them. The breakthrough companies in particular need to learn about the new categories of investors that are filling the void left by the venture capitalists.

The companies offering "iterative" technologies are those creating "next generation" innovations. These are better, faster, cheaper, or otherwise improved versions of existing technologies. These products are easy to understand because the previous version exists, so investors can easily grasp their value. However, these companies number in the thousands, and therefore getting on investor radar screens presents a challenge for them. Still, there are many investors out there who are highly interested in these more cost-efficient, less risky technologies. Therefore, an iterative technology company has to really dig deep to find the right investor fit and launch a cogent, targeted campaign to reach those investors.

When you're framing your message to investors, make sure you're clear with yourself about who you are, what your company is offering, and the type of investors to whom you are reaching out.

Pivoting Is About Measuring Results, Not Activities

So you've sent some emails, made some calls, had some meetings, and experienced some great opportunities to see how well your messaging is working and adapt where necessary. But how do you know if all this effort is getting you closer to receiving an investment?

At this stage, your notes become vital. You have to dive in there and figure out which pivots were effective and which of them went nowhere (see Figure 5.2). You're probably working very hard—making dozens of phone calls, sending hundreds of emails, producing a really cool-looking investor deck—but if you don't measure your results, you can't ever know if all this activity is meaningful.

Have your voice mails garnered zero callbacks? If so, perhaps you should experiment with a more concise voice mail pitch that packs all the relevant information about your company into a short message. Is the new pitch working? Are you getting callbacks now or are you still hearing dead air? Similarly, if your emails generate a lot of clicks through to your website but few positive responses, perhaps an update to your website would turn all that email activity into results.

By keeping a close eye on the metrics for all your outreach attempts—from the number of clicks each email generates to the number of meetings

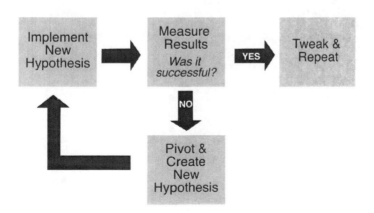

FIGURE 5.2: *The decision tree for pivoting your business*

each method of contact generates—you can home in on the most effective strategies for your company and quickly drop new messaging strategies if they aren't working. Similarly, you can keep more subjective notes on how positively investors are responding to each part of your presentation and retain the slides that seem to work and change the ones that don't.

The purpose of tracking results is to use them to pivot, and pivot some more, until you have an investor in front of you passing a term sheet into your hand. That's the ultimate sign that you have the message right.

Preparing for a Direct Outbound Fundraising Campaign

CHAPTER 6

Branding and Messaging

On a weekly basis, a typical life science investor receives hundreds of emails, executive summaries, and business plans from entrepreneurs who are trying to raise capital. Moreover, many of these solicitations aren't even a remote fit, and the result is a lot of noise and frustration.

There are two keys to getting that first meeting. One is talking to the right people, properly managing your target list of investor fits, and remembering that there are 10 categories of life science investors and you need to map your firm to the appropriate ones. The other is making sure that those "right people" get customized materials that grab their attention and illustrate your value in a clear and concise manner. The fact is that the investor landscape has changed and there is increased competition among emerging life science companies for the dollars that are out there. Attracting investors has only become more difficult, and now more than ever, a focus on branding and messaging is an integral part of the fundraising process.

To win capital, you must stand out from the crowd. The first way to do that is to have top-notch marketing collateral. You must provide potential investors with high-quality, professional materials—materials that engage them, communicate your message clearly and concisely, and present the information they want to see in a way that helps them to decide quickly and easily if you are a potential fit for their needs.

Often investors find the fundraising materials submitted by entrepreneurs in this space to be inscrutable and unclear. Scientist entrepreneurs typically have an academic mind-set; it is common for their marketing materials to include pages and pages of wordy explanations that dive deeply into technicalities. Unfortunately, this often means that the truly useful nature of an asset or value proposition gets lost. The graphical representation of data and performance can't be deciphered, and sometimes even crucial statistics are omitted. When out-of-context logos and distracting colors and layouts are also utilized, investors simply can't understand the message. Moreover, due to the sheer volume of business plans and executive summaries they receive, materials that don't pass muster will likely be discarded. Investors just don't have the time to decipher unclear unsolicited submissions.

In Chapter 5, we elucidated the keys to identifying who you are and how you are different from the rest of the industry. Now you know in what specific way you are offering a great and compelling opportunity for investors, so it's time to put that into a branded package that delivers.

Branding Your Firm

Having a clear and consistent identity and message—or brand—that differentiates you is a critical requirement in establishing yourself as an investible identity to your prospective capital providers.

Many life science executives falsely believe that only consumer goods companies must invest in branding. Many also believe that their technology is so compelling that it will speak for itself. The reality is that branding is equally important in the life sciences, especially when it comes to raising capital, and that selling even the best of products takes some work.

Although you're communicating with a small and highly educated audience, branding influences the choices they make. Your brand is what you present to the world. In creating it, you must ask yourself how you want to present your company and product and how you want to be seen and perceived. Your branding projects an image in the marketplace that is paramount in creating a comfort level for investors today and in years to come.

Your brand identity and message should be showcased in your executive summary, slide deck, website, and all other communications materials that are part of your outbound marketing efforts. This is the minimum amount of materials you need to launch a fundraising campaign. There are many others, such as brochures and newsletters, that can enhance the marketing process. Implementing your identity and message consistently across all written materials is key to building a brand that has positive associations in the marketplace, and enhances your firm's reputation over time.

Developing Your Logo

All leading biotech, pharma, and device companies spend substantial time, money, and effort finding a design firm that will create the perfect branding identity or logo. You should do the same to the maximum extent you can afford. A logo may seem like a trivial component, but it's actually an opportunity for you to create an image in an investor's mind.

The goal of logo development is to create one that embodies the identity of your firm. Your logo is a symbolic representation of what your firm is all about, and it (like your marketing collateral) needs to be clear, crisp, and obvious. Too often, entrepreneurs will pick a logo that is inscrutable to an investor (for example, a complex molecular diagram) without thinking about it from a marketing perspective. You must take the time to consider what differentiates your company from the rest of the marketplace, what values your company holds, and what message you are trying to send. If you take the time to think through these questions, you'll be able to develop a logo that is a strong and simple representation of the image you are striving to achieve in the marketplace.

Your Tagline

Right below your logo should be your tagline. A tagline communicates in one crisp statement who you are and what you do. A common mistake people make is writing taglines that are general and nondescriptive rather than crisp and compelling. Examples of poor ones are "Moving Science Forward," "Next Generation Solutions," and "Creating New Therapies." These don't say anything specific about what the company does. A great tagline explains precisely what you do in a few words and starts to provide the context for who the company is.

Some examples of successful taglines include "Inventors of a Novel, Safe Anti-Cancer Agent" and "Anti-Infective Preventing the Replication of the

Hep C Virus." Life Science Nation's tagline is "Connecting Products, Services & Capital." The tagline needs to capture the essence of what your company does so that the reader has a general idea of what you are about. In the case of the latter example, the company name "Life Science Nation" defines the arena the company plays in. The tagline informs the reader of the company's role within that space.

The Elevator Pitch

The tagline is typically followed by an elevator pitch, which is basically a general description of the company in four to six sentences. The tagline and the elevator pitch should flow succinctly. The LSN elevator pitch reads as follows:

> Life Science Nation works like Match.com. LSN is the premier matching platform for market intelligence and prospect pipeline development. LSN enables life science professionals to generate a list of qualified global targets that are a fit for their company's products, services, and fundraising efforts. The ability to generate these Global Target Lists (GTLs) makes life science professionals more effective and efficient.

Creating a Look and Feel

The look and feel of a brand include the logo, colors, layout, typography—even the style of the graphs and charts—used in your company's communications. In short, everything you use to represent your company's image and information is part of its look and feel. Leaders in winning marketing teams work daily to create and maintain an image that is sharp, clean, and always up to date.

Potential investors see the marketing materials of hundreds of firms that are competing against yours to win allocations. These investors are judging your firm relative to its peers as they read your marketing materials. Some are conscious judgments—and some are not. It is imperative, therefore, to do your research to find out what works and what doesn't, as well as what's new and current versus what's old and out of date.

There is a fine balance to the art of branding when it comes to your look and feel. On the one hand, you want to establish a clear and consistent identity so that investors can quickly recognize your company as you are familiarizing yourself with them and establishing your product in the marketplace. However, times change, and more quickly than you might expect in the world of marketing. What's in one year may be out the next. If you want your company to be seen as both distinctive and current, you have to be willing to review your look annually and decide whether to make some subtle updates.

Beyond the aesthetic reasons to keep your materials looking current and fresh, it is important to accurately reflect the evolving state of your company and the pitch you are making to investors. As we discussed in Chapter 5, you will be constantly pivoting your message—and maybe even your identity—as your company grows and evolves. So naturally, it is imperative that you continually update your materials to reflect this.

It's important to incorporate design elements that other life science companies are using to communicate complex ideas and make them easily understood. For example, I am frequently asked whether charts and graphs should be three dimensional and whether stock photography is acceptable. Such decisions may seem insignificant, but in fact they can substantially impact an investor's impression of a firm.

If your materials follow the principles of branding, an investor will be able to pick up any piece of marketing collateral that your firm produces and know it's from your firm without even seeing the company name. Now that's branding!

Marketing Materials

So what marketing materials are required to fundraise successfully? Figure 6.1 provides a list of the most common. At a minimum, you need to prepare the following three items:

- Executive summary
- Slide deck
- Website

To secure capital, fundraising executives must be more effective at every juncture of the marketing process than they were at the last. This requires putting careful thought and effort into every piece of collateral that you're putting in front of prospects. Most importantly, remember that you are trying to create a persistent presence in the minds of your prospective investor audience. Consistency and clarity of message are paramount.

MARKETING COLLATERAL	PURPOSE	LENGTH
TAGLINE	Distills company identity into a single line	1 line
ELEVATOR PITCH	Explains offering in a short format that can be delivered within a minute	1 paragraph
EXECUTIVE SUMMARY	Briefly conveys opportunity in clear and concise manner	1–2 pages
SLIDE DECK	Provides more detail on offering by expanding on all major points in executive summary	10–12 pages
WEBSITE	Functions as a deep dive sales pitch in an easy-to-navigate, clearly designed layout	Typically a total of 5–7 tabs with subsections as required

FIGURE 6.1: *Marketing collateral overview*

The Executive Summary

Aside from your initial email (which I will cover in depth in Chapter 11), an executive summary offers your first written opportunity to market your company. As the logical extension of your tagline and elevator pitch, your executive summary should flow seamlessly from them. The tagline feeds the elevator pitch, and that feeds the executive summary. A superior executive summary is designed to capture the attention of investors and compels them to investigate further. It is a cogent one- or two-page description that astutely describes your firm and is the first chance you have to make a good impression. The executive summary tells the investor whether you understand who you are and the market. Savvy investors can look at this document and discern who you are very quickly just by seeing how you organize your thoughts and present your company.

Investors know what they want, and if you've done your research on your target investor audience, you'll know what information they expect (such as preclinical findings or a description of the market opportunity). Often just a little bit of investigation will give you a good sense of what makes a particular investor group tick. Focus on highlighting your firm around those factors in an easy-to-interpret format with logical flow.

Though the typical length of an executive summary is one to two pages, be careful not to compress your materials by omitting content too haphazardly. As a wise man once said, "If I had more time, I would have written a shorter letter." This should guide your thinking in creating a brief document that is designed to capture the attention of investors. The most impressive executive summaries immediately give insight into a firm's unique value. They also quickly communicate—ideally, in a few sentences and at most, in a paragraph or two—why an investor should continue reading. If your executive summary fails to do this, your communication will go right into the circular file.

An executive summary highlights key data and information. That is, all the quick facts associated with your firm, such as key asset(s) and technology, competitive landscape, and previous clinical results. Leave out critical elements—or, conversely, include unnecessary information—and the executive summary will be useless. Remember, the point of an executive summary is to showcase your firm and whet investors' appetites.

The Slide Deck

The slide deck is the vehicle that provides a more in-depth view of your company following the executive summary. Remember, you are creating a sales pitch to an investor. Building your message and creating continuity of that message throughout communications is something you need to take time and think about. Moving from a tagline to a four- to six-line elevator pitch to a two-page executive summary to a slide deck should be a seamless process, and each element should be integrated to create a consistent and clear message that is easy to understand. When you have finished creating your message, everybody in your company should be able to effortlessly communicate who you are and what you do to basically anyone, from your grandmother to the scientist consultant who is doing diligence on your firm.

Your slide deck provides you with an opportunity to solidify investors' interest by giving them some in-depth information and data about your company. A common mistake that many life science executives make is to think that "in-depth" means "lengthy." Potential investors will not read a 35- to 50-page presentation, much less one that's 75 pages long. Remember, at this stage, they are evaluating numerous firms for a potential fit. They know that the length and weight of this document does not necessarily equate to the value of the investment. Your job is to efficiently convey why your firm is important. If an investor is interested and needs more evidence or information, they will surely ask for it. However, a great presentation can easily lose its power if it becomes burdened with excessive and unnecessary detail. If anything, an overly long slide deck suggests that the executive did not take the time to distill the information down to that which is most relevant, useful, and instructive. This can quickly translate to a judgment that the executive is "unfocused" or "unable to prioritize effectively."

The most effective slide decks are ideally 10 to 12 pages long. They have a distinct flow, so investors receive the information they want, sequenced in a logical order that's easy to absorb. Too often, entrepreneurs incorrectly assume that investors care only about the data and not the way it is presented; however there are best practices established for these materials.

When creating a quality slide deck, there are several decisions you must make, including how you write your introduction, discuss the firm's management and infrastructure, articulate your science, and highlight the details that differentiate your firm within the marketplace. You also must determine how to highlight information using the most effective visuals. The choices you make represent your firm to an investor and can make or break your opportunity.

The Website

Chapter 7 focuses solely on a company's Web presence and effectively using a website as a fundraising tool. However, I will take a moment now to give you a preliminary idea of how to effectively craft a compelling website.

Your focus should be on clarity, especially when it comes to the layout. Understand that when it comes to your website, your goal should be to present your firm as a compelling investment opportunity, so think of that goal when making every decision about how to structure it. Avoid flashy graphics or filling space without serving a purpose.

The two primary elements that should be immediately visible to visitors are management and technology. These are the two main factors that lead to allocations. Highlight the past success of the management team and academic and industry affiliations, and feature them prominently. Do the same with your technology—showcase how it is differentiated within the marketplace, and take the opportunity to let interested parties dig deeper by providing easy-to-navigate links to papers, publications, and experimental and trial data.

Budgeting for Success

It costs money to raise money. Creating effective marketing materials, conducting a targeted campaign, and diligently following up on communications demand both a time commitment and a financial one. Furthermore, to implement a successful fundraising campaign requires that you make these necessary commitments right from the start.

Many investors tell me they are frustrated by the pitches they receive. Entrepreneurs contact them regularly, hoping to secure millions of dollars in allocations, and yet they haven't taken the time or made the effort to present themselves in a compelling way. What conclusion do these investors draw? Essentially, that these entrepreneurs do not have the business mentality necessary to commercialize their science.

Figure 6.2 outlines some of the major fundraising campaign expenses.

Budgeting for an Outbound Fundraising Campaign

	Required Commitment	
	Time Required	**Estimated Cost**
Developing Marketing Materials & Content		
Executive Summary, 2 Pages (Professionally Advised)	30–40 hrs	$1,000–$5,000
Slide Deck/PowerPoint Presentation, 10–12 Pages (Professionally Advised)	80–100 hrs	$5,000–$10,000
Website (Professionally Built)	200–250 hrs	$6,000–$15,000
SUBTOTAL	310–390 hrs	$12,000–$30,000
Investor Database & Infrastructure		
Quality Investor Database*	–	$7,000–$10,000
List & Task Management Application (e.g., Salesforce.com)	–	$50–$250
Email Delivery, Tracking, & Reporting Application (e.g., iContact)	–	$100–$600
Content Developing Application (e.g., WordPress)	–	Typically free
Ongoing Email Canvassing	40 hrs per month	*Salary Dependent*
Ongoing Phone Canvassing	80–100 hrs per month	*Salary Dependent*
SUBTOTAL		$7,150–$10,850
(Plus Salary)		
Roadshow (9–12 Months)		
Travel, Food, & Hotels	Up to one week of travel per month	If regional: $40,000–$50,000; If global: $60,000–$80,000
TOTAL COST	–	$60,000–$120,000
(Plus Salary)		

A quality investor database should provide about 5,000 global investors across 10 categories, allowing you to filter down to a target list of 300–500 investors that are a fit for your offering.

FIGURE 6.2: *Budget for an outbound fundraising campaign*

Developing Marketing Material

As stated earlier in this chapter, the basic materials required to embark on a fundraising campaign consist of a concise executive summary, a digestible slide deck or presentation, and a high-quality website. Together these materials create a cohesive portfolio with a consistent look and feel and clear messaging, designed with the express purpose of gaining interest from investors. Given the importance of these materials, it is recommended that you engage experts to create them for you. Marketing materials created by professional firms stand out. They look different, read differently, and elicit a different response. They also make an investor's job easier, primarily because they are created with his or her needs in mind.

It may be tempting to create marketing materials yourself. After all, who knows more about your business than you? But as an entrepreneur, you could easily get caught up in the details of the product and lose sight of the big picture. Presentations created in-house are often overcomplicated and hard to follow, and frequently lack the "hooks" required to grab investor attention. By making a financial investment in your materials and hiring expert professionals to create them, you are letting prospective investors know that their time and consideration are important to you. You're delivering clear, direct information, which demonstrates that you know how to market your products and services.

As you can see from the above guidelines, to outsource your initial marketing materials you'll have to budget approximately $12,000 at the minimum. Keep in mind there is an added expense when updating or revising your content. Most companies should allocate $25,000 to $35,000 to account for ongoing revisions and updates. If you have a complex offering, you may have to spend much more.

Investor Database

The global target list (GTL), which will be discussed in detail in Chapter 9, includes target investors that have declared a past, present, or future interest in your product and have capital to deploy. To start with, you should aim to fill this list with approximately 300 unique contacts. LSN has one of the best life science investor databases for mapping current investor interest in your sector and indication. A short phone call to LSN will net you a global heat map of investor interest within minutes. LSN can save a life science executive both time and money and make the fundraising campaign more effective and efficient.

Cloud infrastructure (covered in depth in Chapter 8) will help you to manage your campaign effectively. Email tracking software and a task management system can be obtained for $100 to $600 per year. Using these tools will keep you organized and allow you to gauge investor interest and prioritize accordingly. This will prove to be invaluable when you are in the thick of your campaign and have 16 conference calls scheduled on a single day. Investing in these services is well worth the sticker price.

Hitting the Road

Getting out of the building and calling on investors is imperative. You need to set up meetings and hit the road. A fundraising campaign will span 9 to 12 months or more and may require up to one week of travel per month. The road show comprises the majority of the expense of raising capital; a global campaign can easily exceed $100,000 in costs and over a year of effort. Typically the CEO or the fundraising executive needs to be there. Invest in your appearance, practice your pitch, and create a dialogue. Confidence, focus, and commitment are everything.

Know Your Limits

Creating a budget for an outbound campaign requires an honest analysis of what you and your staff can accomplish by yourselves. Do you think you and your in-house staff can write, refine, and design a top-notch executive summary in less than 40 hours? A slide deck in less than 100 hours? Can you create a full website in under 250 hours? If so, will the content be of professional quality? Will the materials be as effective as they could be? And what other important tasks will not be getting done while you and your staff focus on creating these materials?

Be clear about your own limitations and the value of your time and skills. Do what you can, and seek help with the things for which you don't have time. Don't pinch pennies when it comes to fundraising; make the investment to succeed. Maintain focus, diligence, and an eye for detail; it isn't easy to secure financing.

As I've stated before, raising capital is a numbers game; your best chance to succeed is to source a list of relevant investors (see Chapter 9) and reach out to them by phone and email. The work is difficult and tedious; many attempts at contact might be necessary just to set up an introductory meeting. It takes tenacity and consistency; only persistence will garner results. If you don't feel confident in your company's ability to perform this work in-house, you could consider contracting a third party to contact investors on your behalf, but you'd be wise to first educate yourself regarding these third-party players and the various types of business models they employ. This was covered extensively in Chapter 3 and is a recurring theme in LSN's newsletter, *Next Phase*.

Attracting Investors and Winning Allocations

It's hard to stress sufficiently the importance of marketing materials in today's life science fundraising environment. The competition is fierce and investors are demanding. If you are going to attract investors and win allocations, you must have professional marketing materials. It's that simple. To produce quality materials that are compelling, you must make a commitment of time and money, and then hire the right firm. Just as investors look to you to achieve their investment goals, you must look to marketing professionals to achieve your marketing objectives.

CHAPTER 7

Establishing a Web Presence

Life science company websites run the gamut from eye-catching and professionally maintained to woefully undeveloped and unappreciated. While having a state-of-the-art website isn't particularly necessary, a quality Web presence goes a long way when trying to pique the interest of discerning investors.

In this day and age, no matter what industry you are in, it is an absolute necessity to have at least a basic presence on the Web; without that, your organization will suffer greatly in terms of legitimacy, relevancy, and visibility within the marketplace at large. Life Science Nation's (LSN) experience in researching many early stage life science firms has shown that this is a field where many fundraising executives don't understand the value of having a Web presence. Even among those who do, many lack a full grasp on the website's primary purpose, rendering it a wasted tool. The main function of your website should be to create opportunities to connect with prospective investors.

Without establishing yourself on the Web, you're preventing investors from doing preliminary research on your company. Your site doesn't have to win any Web design awards in order to be effective. However, there is a fairly well-established list of best practices to follow when building a website for your life science start-up, which will help you to deliver your message accurately and in a compelling fashion to potential investors.

Plan Your Website

Before you can launch any effective Web presence, it is imperative that you create compelling content. For this reason, the best way to begin planning a website is to ask yourself some questions about what you're trying to accomplish.

Remember that the main purpose of the website is to showcase your company, management team, product, technology, and clinical data to your potential investors. Essentially your website should be designed as a deep dive sales pitch for an interested investor; it should be a place where all of his or her rudimentary and general questions could be easily answered with just a few intuitive clicks. Your website is the stand-in for you when you are not able to be directly in front of investors to dialogue with them.

Now consider the following: What is the goal of your company? What will investors—both existing and prospective—want to know about you and your company? What else do you hope to accomplish by building this website? Questions such as these will not only give you routes to begin creating content but also help you frame the design of your website and position your online identity.

No matter how you generate content for your website, it's important to remember that unless the information is compelling and useful, no one is going to care about it. You could have the most exciting technology to come along in your indication area in 50 years, but if your website fails to explain that in an interesting and cohesive manner, you will fail to generate any investor interest. Furthermore, the inquiry process doesn't end with initial content creation; rather, you must continue to question your content on a consistent basis to make sure your message is always reflecting the most current state of your company.

After you've developed a fair amount of high-quality content for your website, a good next step is to look around for some inspiration on how exactly to organize it. To get some ideas, check out some websites that you frequently visit. Make a list of likes and dislikes. Do they look professional? Are they easy to navigate? How quickly can you find important information? Keep these questions in mind when designing your website, because these issues will have a huge impact on your site traffic.

With this information in mind, you will be ready to create a site map. A site map is a list of all topics and subtopics that will make up the different pages of your website. Start with the home page, and try to plan a path from page to page that a visitor might intuitively take. In this step, simplicity is of paramount importance; once you have your website established, you can add various navigational complexities, but when getting your website up and running, the best place to start is to organize a simple, logical resource containing all the information a visitor might need (see Figure 7.1).

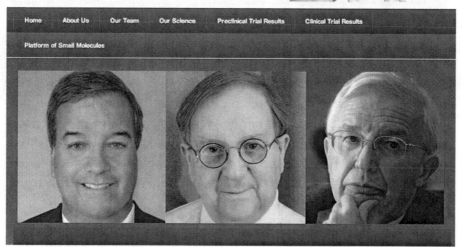

FIGURE 7.1: *A high-quality website layout showcasing the team. Note that all critical elements have obvious tabs that can be easily identified and accessed*

Here is a sample site map for a life science company:

- Home page (Please note: some people set a Home button on the navigation bar, while others link their logo to the home page.)
- About Us/General Information page
- Leadership/Management Team page
- Science/Technology page
- Investor Relations/For Investors page (optional to require a log-in to access this area)
- News page
- Contact Us page

Depending on the structure of your company and your technology, your map may differ, but for the most part, this is how companies within the life science industry (and indeed, many others) lay out their Web pages. At the end of the day, as far as content organization goes, less is more. Keep it simple, minimize distraction, and curate your information so that investors can answer their own questions. Remember, if you think a particular choice could cause unnecessary confusion for busy people seeking information, don't do it. Don't ruin your chance at a precious investor meeting by trying to be original or clever with your layout.

Once you've mapped out your website, you are ready to put your content in the correct places. It is important to note that writing effective Web copy is a specialized skill that requires adherence to some specific guidelines. For this reason, many people choose to hire a professional to edit or rewrite their content so it can function optimally on the Internet. Although this is not necessary, it can be helpful and is something to consider. Most importantly, make sure that your content is consistent with your overall branding and messaging. This means ensuring that there is an alignment of value proposition across all of your collateral.

As you begin to organize your material, try to imagine where you'll be placing any links, photos, charts or graphs, illustrations, or videos to most effectively convey your message. When doing this, it is very important to maintain a balance between all your forms of information; follow your best judgment and only use enough images to make your site engaging and aesthetically pleasing. Too many images create confusion and take away from your message, which essentially boils down to information about your technology and your management team. When it comes to the Web, the more streamlined the information, the better. So don't be afraid to use a picture when it will save you lots of explanation via text.

Whatever you do, your most important priority should be to always use high-quality, professional content. Anything less is likely to raise a red flag, indicating that your team is unaware of how your competitors are marketing and branding themselves.

Do It Yourself or Go with a Pro?

Until recently, to build a website successfully required a clear understanding of website development, the basis of which is rooted in writing valid HTML code. This meant that in most cases the only option for a start-up CEO was to hire a Web developer, either as an in-house permanent employee or as a one-time consultant.

However, thanks to the influx of HTML5 editor websites, such as Wix.com and 1and1.com, these days it is possible to build a website from scratch without any formal training—as long as you have a little time and a lot of patience. The reason I say this is because although websites such as these are widely available and fairly easy to use, they still lack the basic stability provided by those generated through manually written code. This can be frustrating, especially considering that your website is the global face of your company. When you're busy trying to run a business, the last thing you want to do is to be worrying about images rendering incorrectly from computer to computer, text going missing, or worse— server downtime.

Until this technology becomes more reliable, your best bet is still to bear the cost of hiring a professional developer. The benefits of doing this are numerous. First of all, you don't have to do the legwork of developing your website. Secondly, you'll get a finished product that is stable and functional, and visually appealing to boot. You'll be able to focus on the quality of the content rather than the details of the design, and therefore, the value of your site will be more apparent to customers and investors. Most developers will also be able to help you set up email, arrange for Web hosting and domain name registration, and tackle all the other technical intricacies of creating a Web presence that can be a headache for the uninitiated. All of these are great reasons to spend a little extra money and hire the right person for the job.

But what do you look for in a quality developer, assuming you've never hired one before? Here's a list of several questions to consider when looking to contract the best developer available:

- Do they have experience building business websites? Obviously it is a bonus if they've developed life science company websites.
- Can they execute according to the site map that you've created for your website?
- Will you be working with one designer or with a team?
- Do they have references? If so, look into them. If not, find another developer!
- How is their track record for meeting deadlines?
- Are there examples of their design work on the Web? If so, review those sites—not only for quality but also to ensure that their style matches your preferences and ideas.
- How do they handle tech support? Problems will arise; how do they react? This can be a make-or-break issue.
- How do they prefer payment? If they require payment up front, be careful. While some deposit might be reasonable, no professional should ask for full payment until the work is completed.
- How is their verbal communication? Do you understand them when they explain what they do and how they do it?
- How about their written skills? Do you understand the content on other websites they've built?
- Does their work ethic meet your standards?

Essentially, this person is going to be a member of your team, so treat their hiring process with the same care as you would when bringing someone on to your staff. You may end up hiring this individual to work with you on an ongoing basis to keep your website up to date and running smoothly. If this is the case, you'll especially want to make sure you've vetted them thoroughly. Alternatively, if you plan to make changes to your website less frequently, or if you just want to have control over your updates, you can ask your developer to put a content management system (CMS) in place; just make sure you're comfortable with the system and that you'll truly have the time and energy to make the changes when necessary.

If you end up choosing to go with a professional developer, this person most likely already has a preferred set of tools that her or she uses. This will generally include (but is not limited to) Web-hosting software, a secure email-hosting program, and a CMS. Not having to research these options—especially if you have no experience with them—can save you a lot of time and headaches when establishing your initial Web presence, which is just another reason to make the wise decision and go with a professional.

Simplicity Is Key

Whether you decide to hire a Web designer or do it yourself, you must make sure that your Web design is crisp, clear, informative, easy to use, and not too convoluted. As I said earlier, the more minimalist the design, the better. Feature your critical facts prominently; don't lose a chance at meeting with an investor because they can't find information on your team or your technology. You should aim to build a website that conveys both the passion and the professionalism that you bring to your company.

You should avoid at all costs the common mistakes made on many websites in the nineties. Some of these include flashing images, scrolling text, and sound that plays automatically. These elements may sound like enhancements that would attract the interest of visitors to your site, but in reality, they're just distracting. Other pitfalls include using too many colors, fonts, or styles, as well as pop-up windows—these things have all gone the way of the dinosaur when it comes to the current state of Web design.

One problem that I see all the time when browsing early stage life science company websites is that the content is far too complex for the average person to understand. It's easy to see why this happens—many CEOs in this industry are extremely knowledgeable with a deep science background. Often, it can be hard to resist the temptation to lead with an in-depth summary of the science behind your technology. However, time and again, the most successful websites prove to be those that relay the message in a succinct and relatable fashion. Think of it this way: the first time a potential investor in your company visits your website may very well be the last. You need to make sure not only that the right information is accessible, but also, most importantly, that it is comprehendible.

Driving Traffic to Your Website

Congratulations. You've built a beautiful, simple, and informative website. Now what?

As you have discovered yourself by this point, the process of launching a professional website for your company is an arduous one. Unfortunately, compared to the task of generating a buzz around your company's online representation, it's pretty easy. Unless you're lucky enough to have a one-in-a-million technology, or you have the capital available to employ a team that is solely responsible for directing new visitors to your site, yet again, you're going to have a lot of work on your hands.

Having enough compelling content to launch your website is one thing; maintaining it in order to hold an audience is a whole new level. If you have any news or developments as to the progress of your company or evolution of your product, be sure to post updates. Another maintenance task, which is an easy way to promote your website on a small scale and remind your contacts of its existence, is to include links to it in all of your publications, mailings to your potential investors, and postings on the Web.

However, in order to get any real traction on the Internet, you need to tailor the content and relevantly index your material to achieve maximum distribution. This third step is known colloquially as SEO—or search engine optimization—and has recently become critical in getting attention on the Web.

In a nutshell, SEO is the interweaving of keywords and phrases into your website materials that your audience will most likely use to find content such as that which you're producing. In other words, these are search terms relating to your company that would help people find you on the Internet. SEO can be difficult to maneuver, because search engines are engineered specifically to look for websites that are designed to manipulate their rankings and then "blacklist" them, or hurt their rankings in search results. You can't try to trick the system by adding a slew of random, vaguely associated keywords to your materials; it doesn't work and will only damage your website's reputation with search engines. This also means that any claim by a company that they can sell your organization the top spot at any given search engine is false—this rank cannot be bought, because position is organic and never sold.

So what do you do if you want to compete in the world of SEO? The only answer is to be mindful when writing your content, choosing the right keywords for your company and placing them strategically throughout your website, then tagging that content appropriately. (Many Web-hosting companies have a tagging system integrated into their user dashboards, should you choose to host your content directly on their website.) Beyond that, here are some best practices you can implement to help your website climb through the ranks:

- When choosing a domain name, make sure it's creative and specific. It should identify your brand and be unique.

- Avoid using "home page" in the title bar of your home page. It has been shown to lower your Google ranking.

- Create search-friendly titles for your pages that incorporate your relevant keywords (keeping these under 60 characters is best).

- Place individual keywords and phrases in the metatag descriptions. These are built into the code of your design. If you are using a turnkey website, template instructions for this will be included as part of the automation of the template; otherwise talk to your website design guru about this task if you don't have experience doing it.

- Use multiple keywords in a coherent, creative, and compelling way on your website. Most studies show that your best bet for keyword density is approximately 5% for text-heavy pages and approximately 10% for pages with less text. Going outside of this range could cause your ratings to take a hit. If you want to check on your content, you can go to www.SEOChat.com and utilize their free keyword density tool.

- Link every page on your website to the other pages. Search spiders follow those trails to rank your website.

- Simplify navigation by ensuring that every page is no more than two clicks away from the home page (if possible).

It goes without saying that today's Internet is a very competitive place to conduct business. Therefore, you should attempt to make as many connections as you possibly can back to your website. This means you need to do whatever it takes—start a blog, look for partnerships, and register with databases, directories, and search engines. You can also create social media profiles, but don't waste too much time on this; a study done by Outbrain, a Web traffic tool, shows that search is the number one driver of traffic to content sites, which beats social media by more than 300%.[8] That said, without taking the proper steps and having a lot of patience, your website will never gain any traction, so this is one area where you definitely don't want to cut corners.

Testing and Proofreading

Before you launch, it's important that you take every step you can to make sure your website is as editorially sound as possible. The way you do this is first by proofreading and then by testing.

Print several copies of your website and have everyone in your company proofread it. Then have everyone proofread it again, and then do it a few

---

[8] "Study Gives Insight Into Content Discovery Trends Across the Web's Leading Publishers," Kelly Reeves, *Outbrain*, April 14, 2011, http://www.outbrain.com/blog/2011/04/outbrain-content-discovery-report.html.

more times after that. Typos, bad grammar, misspellings, and formatting errors will make you and your brand look unprofessional and detract from your credibility.

I strongly recommend that you also hire a professional proofreader to go over all your site content. Proofreaders are easily found on the Internet, but make sure you check their references and examples of their work. It doesn't cost too much to hire one, and their services are well worth the extra expense; it is extremely valuable to have a fresh, outside eye look over your material, not only to catch subtle errors that others missed but also to point out areas that someone who is unfamiliar with your company, product, or technology might not understand.

Additionally, you should have as many people as you can test your website. They can do this via a test site, which is a copy of your website used for development and debugging. Have them do so from the viewpoint of a prospective investor, a current partner, or whoever else you envision will use your website on a regular basis. All of those testing the site should consider the following questions:

- Do all of your forms and scripts work?
- Does the site work well on all the most recent browser versions? (Take particular caution with this if you're hiring a website builder instead of using an existing template.)
- Does this site work across different devices—PCs, Macs, Android phones, iPhones, iPads, etc.?
- Do all pages have a link back to your home page?
- Do all links work and lead to where they should?
- Are you offering any third-party information or services? If so, you'll need to check frequently to make sure that these sites are still active and that they continue to accurately reflect your brand.

When you find bugs, track them and confirm that you've made a fix. Then retest your entire website. Sometimes a fix can cause another problem, creating a frustrating loop, but one that must be dealt with. So always make sure to test, fix, and retest. A website is a living document and must be treated as such if it's going to stay current.

Monitoring Your Web Traffic

Once you've worked out all (most) of the kinks, you're ready to introduce your company to the World Wide Web. However, even after you go live, there's still work to be done—not the least of which is monitoring your Web traffic. For this reason, you must have a Web monitoring tool in place, and you should also pay very close attention to it. Some Web-hosting companies have their own programs built into the back end of the website; many people choose to use Google Analytics, a free tool that is ultimately the best program available for monitoring traffic.

The reason these tools are so powerful—regardless of which one you choose—is because they allow you to track how many people are coming to your website, who is coming back, how much time they're spending on each page, what content people find interesting versus what's not very interesting, etc. With this information in hand, you can more readily adjust your message to fit the wants and needs of your target audience.

There are a couple of really interesting things that Google Analytics does, which I will mention here. First, it allows you to follow the flow of traffic of your visitors from the page on which they land to where they exit. This is useful because it allows you to adjust your content to manipulate the ways in which people move through your website so you can better direct them to any relevant call to action.

Another very interesting feature of Google Analytics is real-time traffic monitoring (see Figure 7.2). With this tool, you can see from which parts of the world people are currently visiting your site. Since the law prohibits any individual or company from gathering contact information for people who are visiting their websites, this information can prove to be extremely useful. Let's say, for instance, that you send out a targeted mailing to 50 different investors, scattered across different states and countries. Even if a particular investor doesn't click on your mailing (which is the easiest way to know that they're interested), if you see somebody accessing your website in Toronto, and you know that Investor XYZ is located in Toronto, you can fairly confidently assume that Investor XYZ is checking out your website.

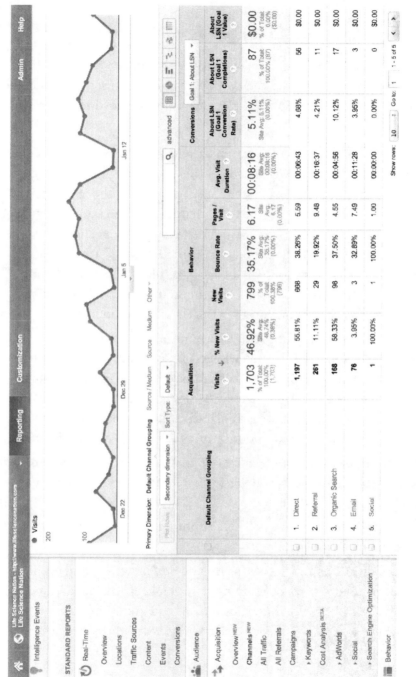

FIGURE 7.2: *Real-time monitoring of Web traffic via Google Analytics*

Keep Your Content Fresh

One of the most important steps in the process of putting together a website is keeping your content fresh; this will ensure that your visitors continue to come back. Fail to do so and you may begin to lose investor attention to your competitors—it's that simple. Here are some suggestions for maintaining your site:

- Keep SEO in the front of your mind, and constantly optimize content you add to your website for the big search engines. Getting your search ranking up is essential to compete on the Web, and you should assume that other life science companies are doing everything they can to progress in that respect—you should be, too! According to a study done by Search Engine Journal, 75% of users never scroll past the first page of results.[9] This is why being very specific in determining the terms and phrases that describe your company (and having a LOT of them) is so important.

- Stay on top of your content. This means never letting it become stale and outdated. Investors will take note of this, and your credibility will suffer accordingly. When something changes, update it immediately; don't wait or you will forget. Remember that the difference between a traditional business and an online one is that your audience is global, and therefore the clock is always ticking.

- Promote your website relentlessly and in whatever way you can. Competition for investor dollars is fiercer than ever, so use your website to your advantage.

- Constantly test your links. There's nothing more off-putting or frustrating than dead links on a website.

- Keep your newsletter, blogs, technology information, and event information up to date. By doing so, you'll keep visitors coming back, which generates analytics, which then allow you to adjust your message, follow trends, and keep up with what's current.

---

[9] "24 Eye-Popping SEO Statistics," Eric Siu, *Search Engine Journal*, April 19, 2012, http://www.searchenginejournal.com/24-eye-popping-seo-statistics/42665/.

Keeping a website fresh is a never-ending task, so settle in! Bear in mind that it's recommended that you reevaluate your website every three to six months.

Summary

In today's marketplace, having a sleek, up-to-the-minute website is every bit as important as having a recognizable logo or carrying a business card everywhere you go. And unlike a logo or a business card, a website must always be transforming. My advice is that unless you already have experience in developing a website, don't try to do it yourself—it is more trouble than it's worth and the end result just won't be as good as it would have been if you had hired a professional. Where your time will be most efficiently spent in building your website is in creating the content, developing your SEO strategy, monitoring your traffic, and keeping your content up to date. Leave the rest to the pros! There is definitely a gold standard for website design, and there are so many aspects to consider that it would be tough to get all of them right on your own. Be vigilant in your content creation and upkeep, your promotional efforts, and your SEO, and with enough time and effort, you'll eventually start making your mark on the World Wide Web.

CHAPTER 8

Leveraging Cloud Infrastructure to Manage an Outbound Campaign

At this point, you probably have a solid grasp of the importance of delivering your branding and messaging to the right audience. Fortunately, there are a range of tools out there to help you do this effectively. In this chapter I will be discussing some methods you can use to regularly touch base with a large group of qualified investors and how you can utilize cloud-based tools to carry out an effective campaign and manage your progress.

Cloud Infrastructure

Before cloud computing became ubiquitous, networks, servers, storage, applications, and other computing resources had to be managed and set up in-house by a start-up company. This was complex and unwieldy for businesses to contend with, costing them an enormous amount of money and resources. Now, rather than having to manage all of those computing resources on their own, companies can rely on software, applications, and infrastructure that is housed in the cloud and shared by multiple users. This has had a tremendous impact on the bottom line for companies, especially start-ups, as it has drastically reduced costs and increased efficiency.

Cloud-based applications such as Salesforce.com can provide you with a fabulous automated list as well as task-management capability for a small monthly fee. Email applications such as iContact are a necessary tool for your outbound partnering campaigns, and you get a lot of compelling reporting for a low-cost monthly fee that will provide insight into who is clicking and interacting with your emails and outbound marketing. Newsletters, blogging, and white papers are another excellent way to reach out to targets to either start or continue a dialogue with multiple potential investors. These cloud apps have created an affordable, easy-to-use campaign management infrastructure that simply didn't exist a few years ago (see Figure 8.1.). These applications are the picks and shovels that can reach the gold the entrepreneur is trying to mine.

A scientist knows that every procedure requires a specific instrument, and if there's a more accurate or cheaper tool available, that's the way to go! We will now cover the various tools available for the key areas of task and list management, content management, and email campaign management.

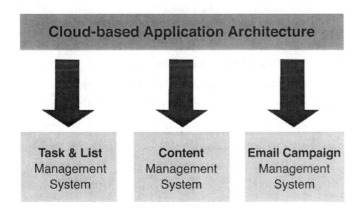

FIGURE 8.1: *Cloud-based application architecture*

Task and List Management

A task and list management system is vital for organizing your communications. I've been shocked to learn that most fundraising executives use convoluted Excel spreadsheets to manage their contact directory, often resorting to a system of multicolored rows, columns, and abbreviations in an attempt to organize their contacts and conversations. This sort of rudimentary solution quickly spirals out of control as your list of prospects grows, and it's almost impossible to coordinate data if it's being used by several different people. One key advantage of using a task and list management system (TLMS) is that it centralizes those isolated bits of data spread across your staff and organization, allowing everyone to use the same system to manage information. This lets you use fewer resources to manage your internal information and streamlines your whole fundraising campaign by enabling you to classify and prioritize your list of prospects and share these priorities among all staff.

Choosing the Right System

There are many TLMS options on the market, and it is important that you choose the one that's right for you. First, make sure to ask whether the TLMS is cloud based; this will ensure that you can access your information from any device that connects to the Internet. This can be vital for sharing data within your organization or for communicating with prospects during a fundraising road show. Secondly, make sure that the system is customizable both in its layout and in the manner in which the profiles are configured, so you can tailor it in the way most suitable for use in your campaign.

The system should cost between $5 and $20 per month per user; it's not a major expense in your fundraising campaign. Salesforce is one of the most popular TLMS options. Although Salesforce has various pricing tiers, their most basic offering (Salesforce Contact Manager edition) should be sufficient for most fundraising executives and is priced at $5 per month per user.

Setting Up Your Profile

Once you purchase a license to use Salesforce, the next step is to customize the system to include the fields you need in your choice of layout. There are some fields that absolutely should be included:

- **Date of Last Email (Date Field):** This should be filled in every time you send an email to a prospect. This will enable you to know the last time you reached out to a prospect.

- **Follow-up Date (Date Field):** This field will tell you the next time you need to follow up with a prospect. By sorting your prospects based on this field, you can track who you should follow up with on any given date.

- **Date of Last Voice Mail (Date Field):** This should be filled in every time you leave a voice mail with a prospect.

- **Status of Lead (Pick List Field):** By qualifying accounts based on the criteria above, you will be able to prioritize your to-do list. I recommend the following categories: Not a Fit, Lead, Cold, Hot, In Play, and Current Investor.

- **Notes:** This is where you can track any significant details from previous conversations. Keeping these notes logged in a central location helps in juggling multiple investor dialogues.

Content Management

A content management system allows you to present content on your website in a user-friendly format. Content can be posted, edited, and deleted via the user interface, providing you with complete control over the process. Some solutions also streamline your site's search engine optimization (SEO) by allowing you to tag your individual pieces of content with relevant keywords; this can make your site more prominent in search engine results. A content management system helps you get your content out there and provides easy access to readers who want to learn more.

WordPress is widely considered to be the gold standard for online content management in the business world; famous names using the platform include CNN, Time, TED Talks, and UPS, and the list goes on. There are many other options, but WordPress has a strong reputation and consistently delivers a high-quality experience, which explains why many big companies put their faith in the tool.

A content management system should also offer easy-to-integrate widgets that will help you engage with users. You can include the ability for users to register for your newsletter or RSS feed, comment on your articles, follow you on Twitter and Facebook, keyword search through your articles, and see any upcoming events that you will be hosting or attending. A content management system should be a multipurpose tool that helps you connect with your target audience.

Content Is King

This is a good place to remind you of the importance of creating high-quality content. Your goal as a fundraising executive is to create an interested audience by maintaining a persistent presence among prospective investors. You have to create name recognition around your firm by engaging your global target list (GTL) with compelling content.

So what is "compelling content"? It could take on many forms, such as a monthly or quarterly newsletter, white papers, press releases, or updates on the development of your products. All of this content can form the basis of an ongoing dialogue with potential investors. However, it can only do so if it is compelling enough to catch the reader's attention and keep him or her engaged. Recycling old information or inundating your audience with dry, boring material will sabotage your initiatives. Crisp, relevant content targeted at the right audience will enable you to establish relationships that last.

Timing is everything in marketing and fundraising. Even though you may be at a too early stage for an investor today, six months from now you may not be, and building positive relationships puts you at a significant advantage relative to competitors who have not done so. This is only possible if that investor has been receiving content from you and is up to date with who you are and what you are doing. More importantly, investors will recognize that you are a savvy entrepreneur because you figured out how to keep them posted on your status without being bothersome or wasting their time.

Remember, investors invest in people first and in products second. When you reach out and contact the investors on your GTL, your content should be showing investors who you are, what your company is about, and why they ought to care about what you're doing. But you also have to develop an infrastructure that deploys and measures the success of your content. Creating, delivering, measuring, and following up are a nonstop, iterative process in the universe of fundraising.

Content Creation—Newsletters and Mailings

Though there are many ways in which an adroit marketer can use email as a creative tool to engage an audience, I will focus on two primary areas that are commonly used with great effectiveness: newsletters and targeted mailings. You are probably somewhat familiar with both. I will go into significantly more detail on email marketing in Chapter 11, but here I'll provide a basic introduction.

Newsletters

Newsletters are regularly circulated publications that appeal to your general audience—in this case, current and prospective investors. This is a chance for you to build brand awareness, strike up conversation in the marketplace, and show your competence in the space. For example, let's say you have a novel therapeutic compound for Alzheimer's. A newsletter from your company could regularly update your constituency on the latest licensing trends in the space, promising technologies that could enable greater efficacy of your compound, or other relevant materials that show you are informed and understand your market position. Data from clinical or preclinical trials, insight into the specific disease area you are targeting, as well as major business developments could also be relevant things to include. This content needs to be fresh and newsworthy; aim to educate and inform your audience, not waste their time.

Education should always trump persuasion when it comes to newsletters. Rifling off a few of your accomplishments is sometimes a good way to gain the attention of your readers, but it is much more likely that this approach will make your readers lose interest. They will read right through it and see what you are doing, which is patting yourself on the back. Also, remember that you're writing for an audience that often lacks a specialized understanding of science. As you write, ask yourself if the content you're producing is going to be engaging and comprehensible to a layperson. If not, it won't serve your marketing purpose.

Targeted Mailings

Targeted mailings can be used more broadly than newsletters, as they are typically custom-tailored messages to a subset of your audience. You might want to send geographically focused meeting requests to all the investors in a certain region in anticipation of a road trip, a mailing targeted at philanthropic investors highlighting the difference your product could make for patients, or any other one-off mailing you can think of to target a group within your audience.

When it comes to mailings, less is often more. Remember that the purpose of your content is to keep current and future investors engaged with your company and updated on the progress of your product. Don't put a whole research paper in the body of your message; rather, focus on providing concise information about your company, your product, and your indication/area of focus. If a certain reader demonstrates interest in your content or a certain article, then you can reach out to him or her and provide more information.

The names of the firm, the CEO or CSO, and the person that is tasked with putting out the newsletter or authoring a mailing should be clearly visible to the reader. The reader should be able to discern one distinct voice behind the message. Remember that investors back people, not just products; you need to reach out to them as individuals. Creating a clear contact person within the firm gives readers who are interested in your messages a chance to reach out.

One final point on newsletter and mailing content: it's better to be safe than sorry. Don't disclose too much proprietary information, and ensure that you're in compliance with relevant regulations such as the Securities and Exchange Commission (SEC) rules on soliciting investors. Make sure to consult your legal advisor and include the proper disclosures in your newsletter or mailing when necessary.

Email Campaign Management

If you're new to email marketing, you may assume that distribution is as simple as opening your email account, pasting in a list of client email addresses, and hitting "send." In fact, sophisticated distribution tools exist that can be much more effective than this manual approach. What you need is a specialized email distribution solution such as iContact, Constant Contact, or Mailchimp. LSN uses iContact, but there are many excellent options available. These distribution tools will track your messages' rates of delivery, opens, and clicks through to your website. You can use this information to gauge which topics successfully generate audience interest and also to perform targeted follow-up with interested readers.

Much like content management systems, the main purpose of these tools is to offer you ease of use when it comes to designing your email campaigns. What used to take knowledge of HTML coding and weeks of work can now be done by almost anyone with a couple of clicks on a "drag and drop" interface. With hundreds of templates to choose from, platforms such as iContact take the effort out of sending professionally designed emails.

And while sending out the latest content from your company to hundreds of potential investors may induce some anxiety, at least the distribution system will make it easy to deliver your email. These providers offer both a spell-check and a spam-check that will warn you if your message is likely to be intercepted by spam filters.

Metrics and Tracking

While producing great marketing content is important, what's equally vital is achieving engagement, and that means you need a way to measure the results of your email campaign (see Figure 8.2). Gather metrics from all of your sources: the back end of your content management system, your email software reporting dashboard, and any other analytical software you're using. The statistics that you gather from your email marketing are very important because they give you information on an individual level. Your email marketing platform will allow you to see the percentage of recipients who opened the email, clicked on the links, or requested to be removed from the list, and even the email addresses of each individual recipient who carried out any of these actions. Email marketing software also often contains analytical tools to graph and compare recipient opens or clicks by location.

The application iContact in particular handles the manipulation and management of all the data your campaign generates seamlessly. You can segment your contacts into particular lists, based on their behavior (or lack thereof) in response to your communication, then structure a follow-up

MAILING REPORT: Newsletter #12

Number of Recipients: 2,500

MAILING RESULTS	COUNT	PRECENT
Opens	976	39%
Clicks	487	20%
Bounces	11	0%
Unsubscribes	3	0%
No Information	1023	41%

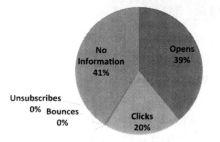

FIGURE 8.2: *An example of a mailing report detailing click and open rates*

campaign to engage users that have actively participated in your mailing. You can also make your own segments that are tailored to your specific needs. One beneficial way to use segments is to perform a comparative test, known in marketing as an A/B test, on your subject lines or message content to two or more groups that are similar in size. This can give you further information on what your readership looks for and exactly what they're interested in.

In addition to their usefulness in testing, segments are good for when you want to target a specific portion of your readership. LSN has used this tool for everything from sending out registration information to specific conference attendees, to touching base with existing customers, to checking in with people we've met on the road.

Deliverability

The most important factor in determining your choice of distribution provider should be the deliverability of your email. Different providers of email marketing software have different delivery rates as a result of how they are regarded by various email servers. The leadership position varies as new providers of both email software and email servers enter the market, so before you pick one, do your research and make sure you're signing up for a reputable provider with high delivery rates. It is worth it to pay more to get an effective delivery tool—otherwise your messages may not reach your intended audience at all!

Subscription Management and Increasing Readership

One of the best aspects of distribution software is automated subscription management. While not very glamorous, this automated process is essential for mass email marketing; if your audience doesn't have the ability to unsubscribe, you are breaking the law according to the CAN-SPAM Act and are putting your entire business in legal hot water. With this tool, as soon as somebody clicks "unsubscribe" on anything you send out, they are automatically removed from your contact list. More importantly, if they ever happen to end up on a segmented list again, iContact will remember that they've chosen to unsubscribe and remove them from the list.

Growing your audience can be a challenge; here are a few tips to help you increase the number of readers who regularly consume your content. First, give your newsletter a name that is less than 50 characters long. Some email software limits the number of characters that are displayed in the subject line of an email, so if your title is not succinct, your newsletter's name might be cut off.

Second, make sure that your newsletter's subject lines are compelling, clear, and reflective of your brand. You must also remember that timing is everything when it comes to distribution. Experiment to discover the best time to send out your newsletter. From my experience, I have found it is best to send out a newsletter when people are typically catching up on their emails; try either first thing in the morning or directly after lunch. It's also vital to make a note of different time zones. If you are based on the East Coast of the U.S. and are trying to target a European audience, you should time your distribution so that your European prospects receive the publication first thing in the morning. With most email programs, you can schedule distribution for a specific day and time, and you can arrange for a newsletter or email to be sent hours, days, or even months in advance. This feature allows you to send out your newsletter automatically so you don't have to be up scrambling at 2:00 AM.

Finally, although it is crucial to build a large network of current and potential investors to whom you can send your newsletter, you need to avoid looking like a spammer. Gaining a reputation for sending spam will cheapen both your company and your brand, and the label has the tendency to stick. Make sure you're allowing people to opt out of your newsletter by putting an "unsubscribe" link at the bottom of the body copy that automatically removes an individual from the distribution list with one click. Remember to always send the newsletter from a specific person's email address or have an individual name attached to the email. This way people won't assume they're getting robotic emails from a faceless corporation; instead, they will feel as if they're being contacted personally by another human being who has something important to tell them.

Summary

There are many tools available to enable a life science executive to carry out a full-scale fundraising campaign. These tools are critical to making your fundraising process efficient and effective. The cost of all of these tools is minimal compared to the value you will yield from them.

Keep in mind that the goal of marketing is to bring you to that ultimate moment: when you reach out your hand and start an in-person dialogue. Also, fundraising is a numbers game, and the more opportunities you have to start a dialogue the better. By using these professional tools, you will see an increase in your efficiency and, more importantly, you will have a better chance of realizing a return on your effort. Now go out there and make it happen!

CHAPTER 9

Global Target List— Match Your Firm with Investors That Are a Fit

Now that you have polished your branding and messaging, streamlined your website, and purchased your cloud infrastructure tools, you are almost ready to begin your fundraising campaign. You have a general sense of the current investor landscape and know who you are, what you do, and where you sit in the food chain of the life sciences. Now you must map out the people and firms to whom you should be reaching out in order to successfully meet your next-round fundraising goal. To do this, you must identify every qualified investor for your company (who could serve both your current and future needs). Live Science Nation (LSN) has mapped out the information you will require to successfully identify and qualify potential investors by generating a global target list (GTL).

Creating a GTL of investors may sound like a daunting task, but it is fundamental to an effective outbound fundraising campaign. Furthermore, though mapping the universe of investors you need to know over the life of your company is a no-brainer, rarely is this task ever executed effectively. In this chapter we will explain how to create a functional GTL of investors for your firm. LSN tracks and maintains an ongoing dialogue with more than 5,000 life science investors across 10 unique categories. These investors' interests cover the full life cycle of a life science company's fundraising requirements, from discovery to distribution. LSN's goal is to uncover a subset of these investors that are a fit for your firm.

The Importance of Fit

Before we go any further, it is vital that we cover the importance of fit. When all is said and done, outbound fundraising is the application of basic marketing principles to the task of raising capital. Marketing is a numbers game, and the metrics of a successful outbound campaign will hinge upon targeting investors that are a fit.

"Fit" means that there is an alignment between your firm and the investor on a number of common factors, be it interest in a certain subsector or technology, indication area, or other criteria. So how exactly do you find the right fit? First, you must ensure that you have a wealth of accurate data, not only regarding prospective investment entities but also other companies within your market. The more fresh, deep, and accurate your data is, the more sophisticated marketing techniques you can employ and the more effective you can be in your campaign. Taking the time to map out the entities that constitute good targets for you will allow you to selectively pursue potential targets that will give you the greatest rate of return. This will set you on the most efficient route to capital.

In the past, a marketer would procure a general list of targets, in this case investors, and take a shotgun approach to that list with various general marketing ploys that essentially amounted to spamming. This method is wasteful and creates a lot of needless noise and activity. Sending an investor that is interested in companies with a focus on shipping medical devices information about a preclinical therapeutic firm is not an efficient use of your marketing potential. It dilutes your message and can leave you dead in the water.

Much better methods are available to a modern marketer with accurate data in hand. If you send a tailored message to a highly targeted audience, you'll get a much greater return on your efforts (see Figure 9.1). If you conduct email marketing using a shotgun approach, your message will typically get you a 1% to 2% hit rate (which measures the number of times the email

Approach	Typical Hit Rate
Untargeted	1%–2%
Targeted *(based on historical activity)*	5%–10%
Highly Targeted *(based on declared investment interest)*	20%–30%

FIGURE 9.1: *Typical hit rates using various outbound approaches*

was opened), while sending out to a targeted list can get you a 5% to 10% hit rate. With more data-driven specificity, these metrics can improve dramatically. As it turns out, in markets with sophisticated target pools, such as the life sciences, a targeted mailing based on fit and declared investment mandates can achieve a hit rate of 20% to 30%. Knowing your target audience and doing your homework beforehand saves time, makes you efficient, and garners superior results.

Now let's discuss the first issue that often clouds a fundraising executive's understanding of fit. There is a myth that the gold standard for fundraising is based on referral (when someone in your network knows someone and arranges an introduction) and that this is the best way to get your foot in the door of an investor. Both utilizing a contact as an access point and approaching investors you don't know but who are a fit for you can be successful strategies. However, it should be noted that referrals often result in what are colloquially referred to as "mercy meetings," where an investor meets largely out of social obligation to a friend, not out of genuine interest. Thus, a company who has taken the time to create an appropriate GTL has the power to trump even the most socially connected start-up.

This may come as a surprise to some, but approaching an investor based on an identified fit is a perfectly acceptable method of fundraising (it's called "selling"). In fact, there are several dangers in relying solely on referrals to engage investors. No matter how connected your team and your board may be, the changing landscape means that there are investors who have mandates to invest in companies they might not be aware of. Beyond that, why limit yourself to calling on a small group of investors that only your friends know? Many investors are looking to expand into new geographical territories or access new technologies. Excluding a potential investor before you have identified their current mandate immediately limits your chance of successfully raising capital.

When you decide to raise money and go after allocations from investors, you have entered the world of selling. If you are raising capital, you are selling yourself and your technology. The sales universe is well established, and has its own proven methodologies. There is no set sales formula, but there are general procedures that work. Be sure as you enter this arena that you don't allow your own bias toward the sales process to deflect from your outbound success in finding investors.

The Importance of Ongoing Dialogue

Before we jump into compiling your GTL, it is important for you to consider that your company is constantly evolving, changing, and moving further along the development cycle. Remember that as you source prospective investors to fulfill your fundraising needs you should be thinking not only about who can fund the next capital raise but also about who will invest in the subsequent rounds. Just because your asset is in the preclinical stage doesn't mean you shouldn't initiate conversations with investors that would be a perfect fit a little further down the line. Having that relationship in place when you need the capital for your phase II trial will be well worth starting the conversation early. This also avoids the guardrail-to-guardrail fundraising approach that causes so many entrepreneurs so much stress and afflicts companies with "fundraising fever" every 18 months. Now, on to identifying your prospects!

A Note to the Reader

In the following sections, you are about to see how we use the LSN company and investor database to determine past, present, and future investment interest in a particular indication or technology. Life Science Nation's offerings are unique in that we have a one-of-a-kind life science investor database containing profiles of approximately 5,000 investors across 10 categories. We are in the business of emerging innovative technology and connecting life science entrepreneurs with investment partners. In the pages that follow, you will see screen shots we have pulled from our database to illustrate our process of uncovering investor mandates that are a fit for our clients.

Defining Past Investment Interest

Remember, investors invest in management teams and products. LSN specializes in tracking investor preferences at all three stages—past, present, and future. One obvious place to begin is to look at where investors have invested historically. This refers to the specific allocations they have made in your sector, stage, and indication area. Take a look at some companies that share similar characteristics to your company. You can find these look-alike companies by using several combinations of major criteria, including specific technologies, indications, phases of development, and geography. This is your comparative landscape.

Let's view an example: a company is developing an antibody-based therapy to treat solid tumors. Using the LSN company platform, we can quickly identify 289 global companies developing preclinical antibody-based therapeutics (see Figure 9.2).[10]

Results 1 – 20 out of 289 displayed.

1 2 3 4 5 6 7 8 ..... 13 – Next

Search filter:
- Sector: Biotechnology – Therapeutics and Diagnostics
- Subsector: Antibodies
- Primary therapeutic area: Neoplasms / cancer / oncology

FIGURE 9.2: *A company search for antibody therapeutics for oncology around the world*

---

[10] Due to licensing issues, we cannot reveal company-specific data in this book. However, should you want to see an example of search content, contact us at info@lifesciencenation.com to arrange a web demo.

This database enables LSN clients to search through a list of over 30,000 companies to find those that look just like theirs in only a few clicks. This capability is powerful because it gives you a global view of your competitive landscape. This helps you identify where your company fits within the marketplace and better understand what investors might see that differentiates your firm.

A glance at the financing history of your competitive landscape will let you know who has voted with their feet and provided capital to your sector, indication, and technology. LSN's platform can be used to identify the lead and co-investors for companies similar to yours. The LSN company database is fed through a network of 45 regional bio-clusters around the world, as well as a network of life science partnering conference providers. Since LSN has over 30,000 company profiles in its global database, a lot of self-declared information is derived from these two channels. Therefore LSN is able to conduct a search of company look-alikes and those who have invested in them.

Let's continue with the example. After filtering the list to include only those companies who have provided lead and co-investor information, we have narrowed our focus down to 134 companies (see Figure 9.3). Typically, LSN will garner 8 to 15 historical investors per company, resulting in a list of approximately 300 to 500 investors. Every investor in this

Results 1 – 20 out of 134 displayed.

Search filter:
- Available information: Financing rounds
- Sector: Biotechnology – Therapeutics and Diagnostics
- Subsector: Antibodies
- Primary therapeutic area: Neoplasms / cancer / oncology

FIGURE 9.3: *A company search for antibody therapeutics for oncology that have declared financing information on lead and co-investors*

list has committed capital and understands the technology and marketplace. (LSN calls this list the "über investor list.") We can now parse that list and do some research on those investors to see how many are a good fit for this particular client. Whether or not these investors end up giving the company any money, they are a great group of people to talk with and be educated by.

This is a terrific way to begin to build your GTL. However, the life science investor space has changed a great deal in the past decade. Many investors have changed their mandates or withdrawn from the space, and new investors have surfaced to fill the void. These are the next entities to add to your GTL.

Determining Present Investment Interest

Once all of the relevant past investors have been identified, you need to determine which investors are actively making allocations to new companies and which plan on doing so in the near term. Determining whether an investor is currently investing in your type of company is a labor intensive process, requiring time, energy, and a high degree of Internet search expertise. LSN has a staff of research analysts who specialize in determining whether an investor is currently investing in the life sciences and, if so, into which types of companies they are looking to allocate capital. These researchers are trained to scour dozens of information sources to determine an investor's current investment appetite. While a fundraising executive like you could learn this process, undoubtedly your time could be put to better use.

LSN has metrics that show it takes 90 minutes of a researcher's time per year to keep one investor profile current. LSN's researchers are dedicated not only to the task of maintaining fresh and accurate profiles for the 5,000 investors in our database but also to finding new investors to add to it. Given the amount of hours this simple but vital task requires, you can see how conducting the initial research would be an inefficient use of an executive's time. Utilizing an accurate life science investor database will save you hundreds of hours and, more importantly, will uncover those investors that you could not have identified using traditional methods.

The LSN Investor Platform is exclusively focused on identifying and profiling the 10 categories of investors that are currently investing in early stage life sciences. (Please refer back to Figure 4.1 in Chapter 4 for an overview of how the landscape has changed.) Taking our previous example of a therapeutic antibody oncology company, we can quickly identify those investors that have current investment interests in that space. From our database of 5,000 currently active investors, we identified 402 investors that have a declared interest for this specific type of company. Significant value is derived when we then exclude all of the VC-based investors—who have already been covered in our search to yield candidates who have demonstrated past investment interest—(see Figure 9.4) and are left with 250 non-VC early stage investors (see Figure 9.5).

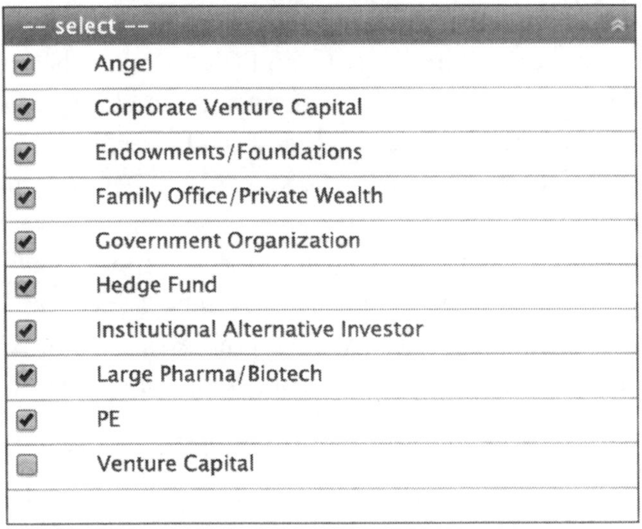

-- select --	⌃
☑	Angel
☑	Corporate Venture Capital
☑	Endowments/Foundations
☑	Family Office/Private Wealth
☑	Government Organization
☑	Hedge Fund
☑	Institutional Alternative Investor
☑	Large Pharma/Biotech
☑	PE
☐	Venture Capital

FIGURE 9.4: *Searching for early stage life science investors while excluding traditional VC firms*

Results 1 – 10 out of 250 displayed.

[1] [2] [3] [4] [5] [6] [7] [8] ..... [25] – Next

Search filter:
- Sector: Biotech Therapeutics & Diagnostics
- Sector Preference: Antibodies
- Indication preference: Neoplasms/Cancer/Oncology
- Investor type: Angel, Corporate Venture Capital, Endowments/Foundations, Family Office/Private Wealth, Government Organization, Hedge Fund, Institutional Alternative Investor, Large Pharma/Biotech, PE

FIGURE 9.5: *In one search, LSN was able to identify 250 non-VC early stage investors interested in companies focused on antibody therapeutics for oncology*

Identifying Future Investment Interest

The final step in identifying potential investors is understanding how they will be investing in the future. LSN's research team has a systematic method of interviewing life science investors to determine their future investment mandates. This information is extremely valuable when building a GTL because it provides actionable information regarding an investor's intended activity in the life sciences.

Investors are inundated with solicitations in the form of emails, phone calls, and business plan submissions. It is up to them to find the best method for sorting through the crush of solicitations to find the opportunities that fit their predetermined mandate; many of those we work with have expressed their gratitude to LSN for our assistance in cutting through the noise of untargeted solicitations.

Building a GTL necessitates understanding the components of an investment mandate (see Figure 9.6). By finding those investors with a mandate that matches your story, you will be able to further refine your target list and dramatically improve your hit rate when reaching out.

Mandate Summary

Allocation Information:

                              is a Family Office fund that was established in 1999 and based in
                                                                    . The firm controls up to $1.5 billion in assets
under management and makes equity investments ranging from $100,000 to academic spinouts to $80
million dollar in later stage deals. The firm operates in a perpetual structure and looks to make
investments around the globe with a focus on companies located within the US and Europe.

Sectors & Subsectors of Interest:

                              is currently looking for companies in both the Therapeutics and Medical Device
spaces. For therapeutics the firm is most interested in companies developing novel biologics however
companies developing small molecules are also considered for investment. The firm is willing to invest in
companies with a product anywhere from pre-clinical to phase III of development although they do require
a substantial equity position into selected companies. For companies with an asset that is preclinical the
firm tends to not get involved if the round is series C or later. For medical devices the firm is open to all
subsectors and indications however they generally prefer to invest in later stage and are not as involved in
the foundation of companies in the medical device space. The firm is not interested in later stage
companies working with primary care technologies.

Company & Management Team Requirements:

Apple Tree considers both private and PIPE investments and strongly prefers if not requires to take a
board seat into portfolio companies. The firm also prefers to lead or co-lead any investment syndicates or
pipes and looks to optimize, not over haul the management team in place. The firm also requires that the
company's management be able to clearly articulate the mechanisms and functionality of their technology.

Message From Investor:

               is unlike most traditional early stage investors in that they look to act as a partner, taking the
company through to commercialization only selling in an M&A transaction if the price is right or access the
public markets, but only if it is advantageous to do so. Interested companies that meet the aforementioned
criteria should reach out to   (Associate) via email at   and
mention LSN in the initial conversation.

Capital Structure	
AUM:	USD 1500.0 m
Investment Stage Preference:	• Seed
	• Venture
	• Growth
Capital Structure Preference:	Equity
Actively In Licensing:	No
Ownership Preference:	• Public Company
	• Private Company
	• Subsidiary

Investment Interest	
Investment Stage Preference:	• Biotech Therapeutics & Diagnostics
	• Medical Technology
Subsector:	Opportunistic
Indications:	Opportunistic
Geographical Exposure:	Global
Orphan Interest:	Yes
Preferred Product Development Phase:	• Preclinical
	• Phase I
	• Phase II
	• Phase III

FIGURE 9.6: *An example mandate from an investor using the LSN Investor Platform*

Components of an Investor Mandate

An investor mandate includes the following important information: allocation information; geographical exposure; sector, subsector, and indication interest; phase of development; management requirements; and a message from the investor.

Allocation Information

All investors have a preferred allocation strategy. A firm will have pinpointed the ideal size, frequency, and deal structure for their investments. In a broad sense, the size of an investment can be linked to the type of investor. Angel groups and government organizations typically invest in small rounds, while private equity firms and large corporations generally participate in large rounds and buyouts. The investment size often corresponds loosely to the assets under management of a company, but as with any mandate, the exact preference of the group must be investigated, as there are exceptions to every rule.

The frequency with which a firm is planning to participate in deals will give you a good indication of how active the investor is looking to be within the next six to nine months. If the firm is not currently active, don't spend valuable time trying to engage them.

Geographical Exposure

In the past, fundraising was limited to the geographical region in which the investor had a presence. Improvements in communication and the globalization of markets have led to many investors taking a more global approach. LSN has seen an emergence of global investors at even the early stages of life science investing. The exception to this trend can be found with regionally based angel groups and government organizations with mandates to fund and attract companies to a particular state or region. Often, investors will make their geographic exposure known; otherwise this information can be determined via a simple phone call to any individual at the firm.

Sector, Subsector, and Indication Preference

This part of the mandate specifies the types of products and technologies in which a prospect is seeking to invest and for what applications. This includes preference for devices versus therapeutics (sector), biologics versus small molecules (subsector), or a preference for certain disease areas (indication).

These preferences can be market, regulatory, or expertise based, and the amount of emphasis on each can vary from investor to investor. For example, indication preferences become central to the investment mission when foundations invest directly in cures for diseases and in organizations with a specific venture philanthropic mission. These investors are looking for the best opportunities to make a lasting impact on the health and well-being of people while still realizing an attractive return. Identifying and reaching out to institutional-type investors with the right combination of preferences relative to your offering is what fit is all about.

Phase of Development

While many investors are willing to entertain a diverse range of technologies and indications for potential investment, it is more common for a firm to invest only in companies and products that have met certain development milestones. These preferences are grouped most often by specific criteria for preclinical, phase I, phase II, and phase III stages for therapeutics, or in the case of medical devices, prototype and clinical stage phases, as well as on the market. Preferences in the phases of development will also roughly correlate with the typical allocation per investment.

Management Requirements

Management team requirements can vary from the generic "experience and proven management team required" to the more specific, such as "only works with teams from the top 10 academic institutions." Conversely, some investors will not have management team requirements, as they may be open to the idea of supplying their own management and technical expertise in the development of a technology.

Message from the Investor

As part of LSN's investor interview, researchers ask investors if they have a particular message to share with the life science executive who will discover and read their profile. This can include further information to assist in determining fit, instructions to reference LSN when initiating a dialogue, and requests to submit solicitations in a specific format. This allows a fundraising executive to get a sense for the investor beyond basic criteria. The end result is an improvement in communication between investors and executives, creating a win-win situation for both parties.

A Word About "Opportunistic Investors"

Though this chapter has focused primarily on mandate-driven investors, as they provide the clearest example of how "fit" works relative to your company, it is important to mention what LSN calls "opportunistic investors." This refers to investors who have an interest in any compelling opportunity and are not interested in restricting where they can allocate. This is another prospect pool that can be approached very effectively with an outbound campaign. Opportunistic investors tend to be savvy and comfortable investing as generalists and have declared an interest in seeing anything that fits just a few criteria points, if any. A mandate for this type of investor might read "opportunistic across subsectors and indications, as long as the company is an early stage asset [preclinical/phase I] with strong management team."

The Best Fit Wins

A savvy fundraising executive recognizes that identifying and engaging potential partners based on a qualified fit is not only the fastest but also the most effective way to engage potential investors. By building your GTL efficiently and basing it on fit, you have the capacity to effectively build a pipeline of potential investors that are aligned with your company's future commercial goals.

Figures 9.7 and 9.8 show how the results of an LSN Investor Database search can be visualized via a heat map. These heat maps show the distri-

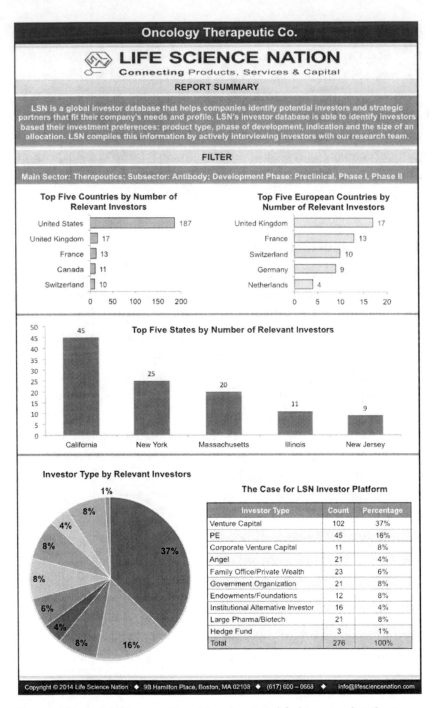

Figure 9.7: *An LSN Investor Heat Map showing global investor distribution for early stage oncology therapeutics*

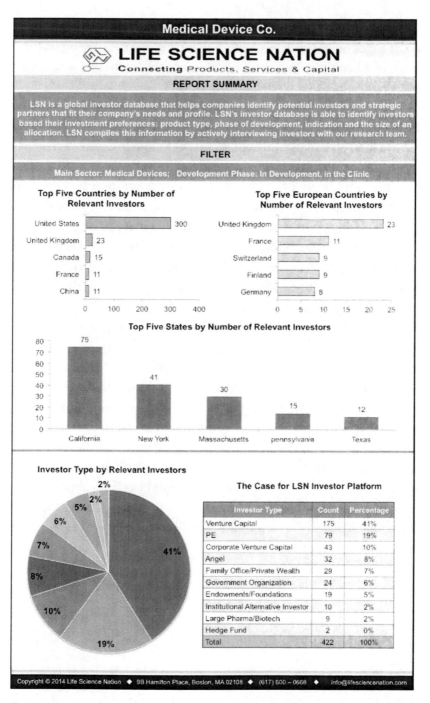

FIGURE 9.8: *Another LSN Investor Heat Map showing global investor distribution for early stage medical devices*

bution of relevant investors for an oncology company and an early stage medical device company, respectively. The heat maps detail geographical distribution and investor type, which can be very helpful in the initial stages of crafting an outbound campaign around a GTL.

Investor database providers such as LSN are a great resource for making your fundraising process more effective and efficient. However, you need to be careful when buying lists and databases off the Web. Data often comes in two states: out-of-date and very out-of-date! So, take the time to understand how the vendors you are working with find, vet, and update their data. Buying a cheap family office list online may seem like a good idea, but if you cannot talk to and get a live demo from a real-life person, it may prove to be a useless resource. Keeping data fresh, current, and accurate is a monumental task that takes lots of able-bodied personnel who know and understand the market. Remember, if it sounds too good to be true, it probably is; you always get what you pay for.

Information is the key to creating your GTL of qualified investors. The public domain holds a plethora of information on life science investors, although some tend to be secretive in nature and will work to keep the individuals and mandates of the firm behind closed doors (LSN researchers are experts at finding them). Identifying historic, present, and future investment criteria is the most effective way to generate potential leads. Sourcing this information for every potential investor is a daunting task that, while valuable, can take up more of an individual's time than is practical. A judicious use of resources should be allocated to build the technical infrastructure needed to source information and manage the qualified leads that will yield your most useful GTL of investors, one that will help you get on your way to receiving an allocation.

CHAPTER 10

Phone Canvassing

For fundraising executives in the life science space, finding an interested investor with capital to deploy has become more challenging than ever, and savvy entrepreneurs must learn to adapt. The types of investors in the life science space have changed, and so too has the ideal mode of outreach by which to start a dialogue with these investors. You need to establish your presence before prospective investors in order to find the right ones for your company, and to accomplish this, you must conduct a concentrated outbound campaign encompassing both email outreach and phone canvassing.

Phone canvassing necessitates a comprehensive understanding of who you are targeting, requires both discipline and patience, and often demands a good deal of training. Phone canvassing is also not for the thin-skinned or for those who lack tenacity, as follow-up is the name of the game. Our research has shown that it can take as many as 10 to 15 calls just to receive one callback and an additional 10 to 15 calls in order to engage in a purposeful dialogue (see Figure 10.1). Even if you make 100 phone calls in a day and only get to engage in a real conversation once, you cannot get discouraged. After all, sometimes it only takes one investor to shift your company from underfunded to cash flow positive, so every meaningful conversation should be celebrated as an achievement.

Relationship Status	Number of Calls to Establish or Reestablish Dialogue
No Previous Contact (Cold Calling, Stranger to Stranger)	10–15
Contacted Once (Conversation Initiated)	7–10
Contacted Several Times (Dialogue Established)	5–7
Existing Relationship (Friends/Family/Acquaintances)	3–5

Figure 10.1: *General guideline for number of calls until contact*

Learning How to Canvass Effectively

Cold calling can be daunting, particularly if it is not something you consider part of your usual skill set. However, it's an essential skill to learn if you intend to raise a financing round for your company. If you are unaccustomed to cold calling, it's normal to find your first calls nerve-wracking. Just the idea of picking up the phone and calling someone they've never met sends many life science executives running for the hills. But even if you don't consider yourself to be a natural when it comes to telephoning strangers, cold calling is something that gets much easier with practice, much like every other business skill you've had to learn in your journey from the biology lab to the biotech industry. It helps if you can approach the task with an open mind and accept that you'll make mistakes as you're learning to canvass; while the stakes are high, it isn't any one individual phone call that will determine your company's survival but a lengthy process of marketing that will involve hundreds or even thousands of phone calls to a huge range of investors.

Even if you have experience with phone canvassing or an outbound fundraising campaign, your skills might need some brushing up or further refinement. Whether you do or don't have experience with this, the people you know in the industry who do can be a fantastic learning resource for you. If you're new to the phone canvassing game, it can be extremely beneficial to listen in on calls with a more experienced fundraising executive at your company; if you're the sole business development (BD) executive at your firm, you may need to reach out to savvy phone canvassers at other firms and ask for a chance to shadow them at work. If you are the CEO of a life science firm and have a science background, then it is best to learn from someone who has more of a business or sales background (perhaps the business advisor on your board). Even if your background is in sales or business, if you're the sole BD executive at a company where every other employee has a background in science, you may want to contact BD executives at other life science companies to see whether there are challenges specific to the life science space about which you must learn.

Shadowing more experienced BD executives while they are conducting a phone canvassing campaign will allow you to understand how your conversation should flow and also how to handle typical investor pushbacks. You'll learn more about the value of your own life science company and how best to pitch yourself to potential investors. Shadowing may also help you feel more comfortable and confident on the phone, especially if it's your first time conducting an outbound fundraising campaign. In addition to observing this executive's methods, you should also be paying attention to the responses that they are receiving from prospective investors. What's working? What's furthering the dialogue? What's landing on deaf ears? After shadowing the canvasser for several weeks, you should be able to discern what separates a good fundraising executive from a great fundraising executive when it comes to raising capital in the life science arena.

Once you have spent a good amount of time listening to phone calls made by fundraising executives, ask them to participate in mock calls with you. You should practice overcoming all the pushbacks that you heard in the fundraisers' calls with potential investors during these practice conversations. Being able to remain calm under pressure is one of the most vital elements of speaking with investors on the phone. Investors receive a lot of unsolicited calls and will try to weed you out; if you are able to overcome all of the hurdles they put before you, you will be able to successfully hold their attention, and they will listen to your company's value proposition.

Researching Potential Prospects

A lot of the vital work of fundraising occurs before picking up the phone. Although the "smile and dial" method of simply acquiring an investor list and calling each number on it may sometimes work, it's more effective to adopt a strategic approach to phone canvassing. Take a minute to understand your target before reaching out. What type of investor are they, and what is their firm's background? What kind of life science companies do they have in their portfolio at present? Have they made any successful life science exits? This information may be readily available on their websites, or you may need to look for media sources that have covered the investor's deals in the past. You also need to understand with whom at the firm you should speak and realize that this person's role or job title may not be the same for every kind of investor.

Many investors have a substantial Web presence. Look at the firm's press releases or the news portion of their website, and use LinkedIn to get a better understanding of who is the right person at the firm to contact as well as a broader look at the firm's structure. Sometimes finding the correct contact at the firm can be as easy as asking an administrative assistant to direct you to the person in charge of deal sourcing or the person who handles life science investments.

There is one pitfall in asking the administrative assistant who is the correct contact, however. Oftentimes this will be a red flag to them, signaling that you've not been in touch with the firm in the past. If they believe that you are cold calling, they are more likely to send you straight to the contact's voice mail or advise you to send an email to a general company mailbox instead of putting you directly in contact with the person. Administrative assistants are often gatekeepers for investors because these individuals get cold calls from hundreds of companies pitching investment opportunities every week. This is why it's best to do your research before calling.

However, sometimes asking for help can get you quite far—if you create a dialogue with administrative assistants and let them help you, you have a chance to build a relationship with them, which may lead to them ushering you through that gateway and introducing you to the person you need to reach. This dialogue could differentiate you from those hundreds of other companies reaching out with their life science business plans. Just know which approach you are going to take before placing the call, and if you are going to enlist the help of an administrative assistant, be prepared to engage with him or her.

Before you start calling, you should not only know the contact's job title but also try to discern the individual's role in the due diligence process for life science investments and ensure he or she is the person who evaluates investment opportunities. Sometimes you can easily figure out the right person's role from his or her title. For instance, at private equity firms, the person whom you will want to contact will generally be a VP or associate who specializes in life sciences, as these individuals are usually in charge of deal sourcing and typically consider investment opportunities in your sector. However, sometimes the person who plays this role is much less obvious, especially in the case of family offices. Thus, you should always check the investor's website to see if there is a description of this role; if not, look at how positions are categorized on LinkedIn. Sometimes even checking the groups in which different employees are members on LinkedIn can yield useful clues.

After doing some research on the person with whom you are trying to get in contact, the next step is determining the best time to reach this person. Catching the individual at the right time of the day is key; although this may seem obvious, you should first check what time zone he or she lives in. If you don't know what city he or she lives in but do have a phone number, you can Google the area code or country code and then check the time in that city or country. If you're reaching out to international investors, you may need to alter your own usual work schedule in order to have a chance of catching the people with whom you need to speak.

You must also be mindful of lunch times and summer hours. Many investors are difficult to reach between the hours of 11:00 AM and 1:00 PM or 12:00 PM and 2:00 PM, as they may have lunch meetings. Conversely, some investors may eat lunch at their desks, hoping for some peace and quiet while their colleagues are out, so it may be worth your while to try to contact someone during typical lunch hours. It can also be difficult to reach individuals late in the afternoons on Fridays, especially in the summer, so it is best to try to structure your call times so as to reach out to individuals in the morning or early afternoon, if possible.

Be aware of cultural norms affecting work schedules. In the Middle East, investors only work Sundays through Thursdays, so you should not reach out to investors in this region on Fridays. In Spain, lunch is the largest and most lengthy meal of the day; therefore lunch breaks last longer than they do in other countries. In parts of Europe, pension funds and government organizations close at around 3:00 PM, while in the U.S. they typically close at 5:00 PM. It is important to keep all of this in mind when reaching out to investors.

Being cognizant of holidays is also vital. There are several U.S. federal holidays, but also a few more obscure holidays that are observed on a state-by-state basis. The top U.S. hubs for life science investment, Boston, San Diego, and San Francisco, share many of the same holidays, but Evacuation Day is an example of a holiday that is only observed in Boston and some surrounding cities. Other countries obviously observe their own national or religious holidays. Dates for state and national holidays can be easily found online.

It can be hard to reach investors during the summer. This is especially true of European residents. Unlike in the U.S., every European country has statutory minimum employment leave, usually over 20 days per year (though leave may be paid or unpaid). Long summer vacations are therefore quite common. Also keep in mind that many people may use statutory leave days to take a break in December.

Staying Focused

It takes commitment to be a phone canvasser. If this is a new role for you, it may help to keep in mind how important this is for your company; the vital scientific work that you're doing will reach the market and have an effect on patients' lives only if you can raise enough funds to keep progressing. That means you have to focus on the campaign above all else. Ignore distractions, and try to avoid multitasking; you'll do better on the phone if you put all your energy into the task and get into the zone. Learn as much as you can from the new experience and take pride in your ability to create a dialogue with investors. Your positive energy and enthusiasm will be evident to the prospective investors with whom you are speaking; one key factor many investors value is the management team's commitment to the company, so it's vital to demonstrate to investors that you have a passion for what you do.

Structure your time; if you have other responsibilities within the company, make sure a certain portion of your schedule is dedicated to simply making calls. If you stay focused and your contacts are well organized, your number of calls per day can increase to 20, 30, and perhaps even as many as 50. As I said before, phone canvassing is by nature a numbers game; the more calls you make to qualified, well-targeted investors, the more likely you are to make contact with someone who has an interest in your company.

Streamlining Your Pitch

The most important stage of your campaign planning process will be deciding how best to pitch your company. If you're speaking to someone who's pressed for time and who has already received 100 cold calls from life science fundraising executives that week, how can you make your company stand out?

Your first step is to draft a concise and powerful elevator pitch that encapsulates who you are, the reason for your call, and your distinctive value proposition—in short, what makes you distinct from your competitors. Keep it short and to the point; your initial pitch ought to be around one minute long. The person to whom you are speaking has a thousand things to get done during the day, and listening to your pitch is low on his or her priority list. By being concise, you're demonstrating that you respect the person's time and you know how to make the most of that brief span of attention. Hit on the key points and offer to follow up by email with your 10- to12-page slide deck so he or she can learn more about your company. You should practice your pitch and be prepared to go off script to answer questions; try to avoid sounding stilted.

One common pitfall in life science fundraising is jumping immediately into the technical minutiae of your product during your pitch. That's not going to engage most investors and certainly isn't the best use of that one minute of time that they're offering you. Instead, think of your pitch as an introduction of yourself and your company, and describe your scientific work in engaging, accessible terms. If they're interested in your pitch, you'll have an opportunity to share your scientific results with them at a later time.

When creating your pitch, you must also be specific regarding fit; you can't follow the same script for each investor. Emphasize qualities that you know the investor values, such as a novel technology, a large potential market, or a shorter timeline to regulatory approval. You need to figure out how your interests are strategically aligned with the investor's interests. One way to do this is to look at the investor's current portfolio of companies and determine whether an investment could be complementary to the firm's current portfolio or could help to diversify the investor's current holdings. Stress how your firm is a fit for their interests; this will lead to a more meaningful dialogue and will undoubtedly make you more successful in gaining the investor's interest in your company.

Once you have your pitch down, it's time to call the investor. You need to be extremely on point and attentive to the investor's mood. Often investors may sound short or rushed on the phone. If this is the case, then you need to make sure that you cut to the chase in terms of your value proposition. If the investor sounds cheerful, then a lengthier approach may be appropriate; feel free to go off script, and respond to any comments they have. Just as no investor is the same, no conversation will unfold in the same way; being able to adapt quickly to the tone of the call is invaluable.

However, often the hardest part of the process is reaching the investor directly. You're unlikely to find someone sitting at his or her desk waiting to take your call. It's more likely that you'll be connected to the investor's voice mail, or that their executive assistant will offer to take a message. It's generally worth leaving an introductory voice mail, as an interested investor may very well call you back; however, in a voice mail pitch, you should be prepared to be even more succinct than you are in your usual elevator pitch. Try to keep it down to 30 seconds in length; at the end ask the investor to call back as soon as possible and tell his or her you're sending a follow-up email. Make sure the follow-up email includes all your contact information and a request to set up a time for a callback; busy people are more likely to respond to you if you propose an appointment within a specific time frame than if you leave an open-ended "Please get back to me." At LSN, we've found that many investors, particularly large institutional investors, are easiest to reach if you use email to set up a date, but of course it never hurts to call first and see if you can catch them in person.

Unfortunately, most people will not respond to that first voice mail or email. Don't let this come as a surprise to you or as a signal to go elsewhere. Lack of response to a first attempt doesn't mean that the investor isn't going to be interested—he or she might simply have been too busy to respond yet, or your correspondence could have been lost under a mountain of other work.

To be successful at raising capital, you must be determined. This doesn't mean that you should be pushy, but it means you need to be very diligent in your follow-up process. If you haven't heard back from an investor after two or three days, you need to give him or her another call, and again leave a voice mail (see Figure 10.2). The message you leave should reference the last voice mail that you left, as well as the follow-up email that you sent previously.

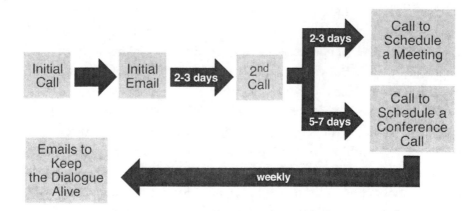

FIGURE 10.2: *Example of how to structure your canvassing efforts*

If the person you're trying to reach has an administrative assistant, don't fall into the rut of leaving repeated messages with that person in call after call. Instead, try to start a dialogue; note down the assistant's name and be sure to address him or her by it. Start a conversation and express interest in the investor; perhaps you can sympathize with his or her heavy workload and ask if there's a better way to reach out, such as by sending an email or scheduling a conference call. The administrative assistant may open up after you engage him or her in conversation and give you valuable information that will help you contact the person the next time you call. As a fundraising executive, you need to think outside of the box in order to get the right person on the phone; it's often not quite as simple as just dialing a number.

The Essential Follow-Up

Following up with targets is one of the most essential aspects of phone canvassing. Fundraising is an extremely time-consuming and lengthy process. It's easy to get caught up in a very good conversation and think that an investment is right around the corner—all you need to do is sign the dotted line, right?

While being optimistic about the fundraising process will certainly help you to keep your sanity, you should not underestimate the time that it will take for you to achieve your goal. A normal fundraising time frame is 9 to 12 months. A very lucky company might see an investment in as few as 8 months, an unlucky company might work for 18 months before receiving an allocation, and, of course, many fundraising campaigns won't result in an allocation at all. But you can greatly increase the odds of getting an allocation if you embrace the marketing process.

The goal of your fundraising campaign is not only to get cash but also to find the right partners to help you grow your business. Therefore the purpose you should keep in mind while phone canvassing is to establish a professional relationship with the investor. Even the investors who speak with you that are not a fit today may be a fit down the road; perhaps they want to see you hit certain milestones before they'll consider an investment. You also never know whom that investor may know; if you keep up a dialogue with interested investors who don't want to invest at present, they might offer you a referral to other firms with whom they've syndicated or made deals in the past and whom they know to be a better fit for your present profile than they themselves are.

How you follow up will depend largely upon your current relationship with the investor, his or her level of interest, and where you left off in your last conversation. Below are some possible outcomes with tips on how to handle your follow-up procedure. It is important that you establish a schedule for follow-up and stick to that plan; a consistent plan will help you to keep your prospects organized and ensure that the entire process is streamlined and efficient. Make sure you have up-to-date contact information for everyone to whom you're reaching out, including their present title, direct phone line, and email address.

Now for the possible outcomes:

- You speak with an investor and have a great conversation. This is, of course, the ideal situation. If this happens, then a follow-up call should be scheduled, or even a face-to-face meeting. You should not delay in following up; rather, it's best to set a date for follow-up at the tail end of the conversation. You should also email your investor deck and any other supporting materials that may be interesting to a potential investor immediately upon completion of the call, if you haven't already sent them.

- The investor is interested but doesn't seem highly compelled. In this case it is wise to follow up periodically. The ideal frequency for these check-ins will vary per investor; you want to be attuned to his or her preferences. Push it when you can, but in other cases be willing to have patience. Make sure before you conclude your phone call that you find out a general time that is good to reach him or her and coordinate a time to speak in the future. Also, you should try to see if he or she will be in your area at some point or attending any networking events or conferences that you could also attend. Face-to-face meetings are always more ideal than conversations over the phone; perhaps meeting this investor in person could lead to his or her mild interest turning into serious interest.

Thus, you should never pass up an opportunity to meet an investor in person, even if you believe he or she does not have a strong interest in your company.

- The investor seems to have little to no interest. If this is the case, it is important to find out why to help you determine whether attempting to maintain the relationship is worthwhile. Even though this may be extremely discouraging, it is still important to remember that valuable information can be obtained through every conversation, even if you get negative feedback.

  - Perhaps he or she is not interested in your particular disease area or not familiar with the indication you are targeting. If this is the case, then attempting to prolong the dialogue is probably not worthwhile. You should certainly make note of the points the investor found less compelling, because you may learn some valuable information about how to approach investors in the future that have not previously invested in your product's disease area, but then be sure to remove this investor from your global target list (GTL).

  - If he or she *is* interested in your disease area or indication, you must still have the courage to ask what it is about your company or pitch that turns him or her off. This requires toughness and the ability to hear constructive criticism. Although occasionally the cause of his or her disinterest might be out of your control (for example, the stage of your company or your particular management team might not be a fit for them), don't be tempted to make assumptions about the reason. Listen to him or her then use the information you receive to pivot your message or tweak your pitch and materials.

- The investor has an interest in your technology, but you do not have enough clinical data for his or her liking. If this is the case, then it is appropriate to follow up later down the line when you do have sufficient data. You should make sure to keep this investor on your list and email him or her when you have collected new positive data.

Gauging the type of follow-up that is appropriate thus hinges upon the amount of interest an investor expresses and your current relationship with the investor. You need to stay organized during this process and keep excruciatingly detailed notes. Don't try to force an investor's interest, and keep in mind that fit goes both ways. Try to structure your time in an efficient way and spend the majority of that time starting or keeping up a dialogue with investors who are legitimate prospects.

Summary

Phone canvassing can be one of the most effective ways to reach out to investors—if executed properly. You need to remember to stay focused, work hard, and, above all, stay optimistic. Know that it is a numbers game, so the more investors you engage the more success you will have. Focus on the positive conversations, not the negative ones. There is a perfect investor out there; your job is to find him or her so you can find cash for your company.

CHAPTER 11

Email Campaigns

One of the most valuable and cost-effective tools that can be used to create a successful fundraising campaign in the life science space is email marketing. It allows you to introduce your firm to potential investors inexpensively and on a scale unmatched by other forms of outbound marketing.

The ease with which anyone can develop and execute an email marketing campaign also makes it one of the most widely used—and abused—tools in the industry. This broad usage has not only created a lot of noise but also a great deal of spam. The challenge for your firm is to create an effective email campaign that stands out from the crowd and avoids the "spam" moniker.

The Benefits of Email Marketing

Email marketing is an excellent way to introduce your firm to new investor prospects. "Introduction" is the operative word at the beginning of any fundraising process. An introduction means a meeting to introduce your firm's executive team, products, and services—not a direct solicitation for capital. The obvious benefits of an email campaign are breadth of coverage and efficiency regarding time and resources; you can reach a large target audience in less time than it would take to carry out a phone canvassing effort, and email marketing is much more economical than a snail-mail campaign. No other form of marketing gets your message in front of larger pools of prospective investors in less time and for less money than email. However, to launch an introductory fundraising effort via outbound marketing requires awareness of the regulatory compliance issues—this can't be stressed too much.[11]

Email marketing is typically used to deliver a direct message. For example, an email blast is an ideal way to lay the groundwork for a road show. An initial email can announce an upcoming trip, deliver all the key facts about your firm, and explain why a meeting might make sense. Email can also be used as an icebreaker. Some prospects may need to hear more before they commit to an introductory meeting. For those investors, email campaigns open the door, making it easier for marketers to place calls and begin conversations.

In short, email marketing has four primary advantages for fundraising executives over other types of outbound marketing. Together, these features make for a devastatingly effective combination:

- **Broad Coverage:** It is easy to hit massive groups of prospects on a broad geographical basis.
- **Highly Customizable:** It is easy to control content and adapt messaging for various audiences.
- **Trackable Analytics:** It is possible to gain real-time insight on key target client groups and gauge their interest levels.
- **Inexpensive:** Email marketing is relatively cheap and doesn't require any significant investment in infrastructure to execute effectively.

Fit Versus Referral

The importance of fit when it comes to targeting potential investors was covered extensively in Chapter 5 and Chapter 9, and it is worthwhile to bring it up again here. The issue of fit versus referral is one of the most mis-

---

[11] Refer back to Chapters 1 and 2, which state the rules regarding outbound solicitation and accredited investors.

understood parts of the fundraising process, and countless companies fail to raise money simply because their fundraising executives won't believe that a cold email can be effective. However, it has been proven time and time again that cold emails with diligent follow-up targeting the right group can be extremely effective. This is primarily because with cold emails you can immediately reach exactly the right people in the investor organization, and that makes a significant difference in gaining investor interest. You need to reach the right people, not just the right firms.

Too often, companies raising funds rely on the belief that an introduction by a friend of a friend to a senior level player within an investment entity is effective. This certainly can be the case sometimes, but typically, these introductions take up lots of resources and lead to the wrong individual. There is a good chance that this person isn't "in the know" regarding the life science investments his or her firm is making, but he or she will usually take a meeting with you to be kind. Afterwards, he or she will try to refer you to someone else, who quite possibly isn't the right contact person either, and so on. You may spend a great deal of time in contact with the wrong people in the company, only to discover ultimately that the investor wasn't a correct fit for you to begin with. This is a waste of time and resources and can hold you back from achieving your fundraising goals.

A fit can be thought of as a self-referral based on stated criteria. Using a list of firms and individuals that are a strong fit can be incredibly effective, because it prevents you from being seen as an obligation. Instead you approach the firm as person with a company and product that they are actively interested in. That's a much more powerful initiation of contact than a mercy meeting that is doomed to be unproductive.

Managing Your Global Target List

Before you start your email campaign, you will want to take the global target list (GTL) of potential investors you've already come up with (see Chapter 9 for more information on this) and segment it into different sub-lists. While there are occasions when it will be useful to send one email to your entire list, more often you will want to tailor your particular marketing efforts to a specific group, and for this you will need to create segmented lists. For example, if you are planning a road trip in a specific geographical area, you should create a segment from the master list for that campaign.

After you have segmented your GTL, the next step is to put the data into a manageable format. Data comes in all types of formats—particularly if you purchase lists—so for ease of use and quick reference it is important to get it into one you can work with most easily. Most bulk email service providers, as well as internal email programs, manage data in the comma-separated values (CSV) format, which can be manipulated and managed in Microsoft Excel.

Using Excel, separate the data into columns. Use separate columns for first name, last name, email address, company name, city, state, and country. In addition to the contact information, create columns for any other pertinent data that helps to screen investors moving forward. Putting the first and last names in separate columns gives you the flexibility to personalize greetings using a mail-merge option. I have always found that using first names in messages delivers the best response; using first and last names seems to flag your message as being a processed email. Also bear in mind that for email campaigns, it is important to organize the data by contacts, not companies, for ease of manageability.

A simple yet common mistake many marketers make is inputting the data as-is, without conforming the formatting. You must make the data uniform. Some list providers may have names set all capitalized; others use upper- and lowercase. Some include courtesy titles such as Ms. or Mr. and professional titles such as Dr.; others don't. You should make sure the format is consistent and that no entries contain random characters or capitalization. Also, make sure to put titles in a separate column rather than as part of the name. You don't want to find yourself sending an email that begins with the greeting "Dear Dr. Bob." Furthermore, inconsistencies can cause problems later with mail-merge options and email applications.

If you've downloaded data into your spreadsheet, make sure it matches up across columns. All it takes is one mix-up when downloading the data to misalign the contact information. Eyeball your list. Does everything line up? Look for names you know. Is their contact information correct? Do the contacts' company names match their email addresses? I can't tell you how many times I have sorted a list and been ready to upload it to my email software only to realize that the names and email addresses are off. Nothing kills the potential for an email blast faster than calling recipients by the wrong name. It makes it clear that they are on the list of a firm that operates hastily.

The next step is to review the recipients on the list and remove all those prospects who, for whatever reason, should not be receiving your email. For example, if the purpose of the email campaign is to request a meeting to introduce yourself and your firm at an upcoming marketing road show, it would not be appropriate to include current investors or firms that know you well. If you want to meet with prospects you know, those meetings should be scheduled by making direct contact, either by phone or email. In addition, if you have prospects who have asked to be removed from your list, you need to honor their request. Nothing will turn off an investor more than receiving repeated and unwanted solicitations following requests to be removed from your list.

As you review the names on your list, you also need to be cognizant of the relationship you have with the contacts and their firms. If an investor official from a small institution, such as a family office, requests not to be contacted, his or her decision may also cover the remainder of his or her team because of the high likelihood of close collaboration. Sometimes though, the person opting out is low on the food chain within a large organization. In this case, you, as a savvy marketing professional, may decide to keep this person's boss on your list, as he or she may see your offering and decide a meeting makes sense. Coming into a firm through another channel or at a higher level sometimes makes the difference between getting a meeting and getting no response.

One question that often comes up when it comes to email campaigns is who should be contacted at a large firm with multiple points of contact listed? Moreover, if you don't know who evaluates potential investments, should you send an email to all the contacts listed? These questions fall into a gray area—an area that fundraising executives often find themselves in. Your goal is to reach an audience that is large enough to achieve your targeted hit rate. At the same time, you don't want to dilute the impact of your email by sending it to the wrong people within an organization.

The answer is: do your homework. Find the right person. This is imperative, because ultimately, fundraising is relationship driven, and you do not want to burn your firm's brand capital by appearing to be too cavalier with your efforts. As a life science firm marketer, you must reach out to enough people to ensure that your message reaches investors who are a fit while always being aware of the way your message is being received by your prospects.

Launching Your Campaign

After your list has been vetted, screened, and pruned, it's time to select an email software program through which to deliver your messages. Email marketing software platforms allow you to easily upload and manage your email list, create email messages, and send them. If you created a list in a program such as Excel, you can upload it to an email marketing platform offered by a company such as Constant Contact, iContact, or VerticalResponse, greatly reducing the time and effort it takes to produce and distribute the many emails associated with your marketing campaign.

We have already gone over the many benefits of using email marketing software (see Chapter 8). In addition to offering high rates of deliverability, monitoring tools, and analytics, this software gives you the ability to manage the opt-out requests of your recipients. Although the emails are sent through the systems' own email servers, all messages appear to be coming directly from you, and all responses from the recipients are sent directly back to you. However, these systems include opt-out links and manage the responses.

The opt-out link is usually located in the footer of the email. Not only must your email include this to avoid being considered spam, but the link is efficient for the folks receiving your email. When recipients opt out, usually these platforms let them specify the types of messages they don't want to receive. Then the platform implements their request to make sure that they are not unwittingly included in any other email campaigns. In fact, many platforms never allow that contact back on your list, thus saving you from accidentally uploading a list that includes that recipient in the future.

Another great feature of these email software platforms is the "schedule delivery" tool. This allows you to create an email message and choose the day and time it will be sent. I use this feature often. It lets me create an email campaign during normal work hours in the U.S. and then schedule it to be sent at another time, for example, to London prospects at 4 AM (EST). There's no need for me to be up at that hour to hit the "send" button. This little option allows me to prepare a campaign when the creative bug hits, schedule it, and then forget about it.

Types of Mailings

Within the realm of email marketing campaigns, most messages can be divided into one of the following three groups:

- Introductory emails
- Announcements
- Newsletters

Introductory emails are the focus of this chapter, as we are outlining the process of initiating a dialogue with an investor audience. However, I will briefly cover the other two, because they become critically important when it comes to maintaining a dialogue once it has been initiated.

Announcements and newsletters are two great ways of generating "buzz" and "draw." This essentially means creating a persistent presence in the marketplace so that your firm becomes a "household name" among your target audience. Announcements and newsletters can be used to build anticipation before major events for your company and to create a following that has a legitimate interest in your firm's progress.

Announcements are used to alert an audience that knows about you and your firm to major events surrounding your firm. These can include that you will be attending or presenting at an upcoming industry conference, that you've hit a milestone in the development of your product, or that you've closed a financing round. These mailings can be important sources of inbound leads (people replying directly to the mailing) as well as passive leads (people who have clicked on links, attachments, or other content that your email tracking software is able to monitor). Keep these regular but don't overwhelm your audience. Sending one or two announcements per month is a good idea to begin with; once you get more information on how your audience is responding to them, you can pivot from there.

Newsletters are used to maintain a dialogue with a readership and can be a powerful way to stay engaged via a passive, less overtly sales-oriented tool. Content often covers industry trends, but you can also connect with your readership through a novel, credible view of an industry issue. However, it is critical to ensure that your content is interesting, insightful, and edgy while not discrediting your firm; thorough fact-checking is a must. Innuendo, hyperbole, and false statements can really hurt your brand, so speak from a knowledge base and ensure you can add concrete value with your communications. Given the effort required to maintain a newsletter on an ongoing basis, a fundraising executive should consider whether it is something that can be sustained.

Should you decide to send out a newsletter, it is vital to include clickable content that allows targeted trackability of readership. The screenshot of an Live Science Nation (LSN) newsletter (see Figure 11.1) indicates all of the clickable elements within the first page alone.

Newsletter Layout

All the newsletter creation applications I have sampled offer the basics, including formatting and spell-checking. Many also offer advanced features that allow for embedded links and HTML design. In fact, the three providers mentioned earlier (Constant Contact, iContact, and Vertical-Response) collectively offer more than 200 templates to help you get started. Or you can create your own using their "quick start" options, which allow you to keep the template simple, so you can skip directly to writing the body.

Make sure to create a layout that optimizes the ability to track and capture user information. Create embedded links and prompt users to click on them to visit your website and find additional information such as your executive summary. When your recipient clicks on one of your embedded links, your email software will alert you and provide you with his or her relevant contact information. This is powerful information, as it allows you to identify investors that have responded to your message by displaying an interest in learning more about you. Refer back to Figure 8.2 in Chapter 8 to see an example of a click report from a mailing.

To fully benefit from this feature, you must be deliberate in your layout of the links. Make sure your links are visible within the opening of the email; oftentimes they are embedded deep into an email, which generates minimal user interaction. Second, embed different types of click options, such as buttons or hyperlinked text, because these elements allow you to track reader behavior. Third, links should be highlighted to bring attention to their existence.

Generating Clicks

Each element indicated by an arrow on the graphic on page 154 (Figure 11.1) is an example of a clickable link. Each click will automatically populate an Excel sheet with as much information as you have associated with each contact. Through no effort on your behalf, this becomes a lead sheet that you can use in following up and starting a dialogue. The best way to entice a click is to keep your content fresh and relevant, while giving your audience just enough information to want to keep reading the article or blog.

The Subject Line

Now let's tackle the creation of the email and its two key components: the subject line and the message. The subject line is the first thing your recipients see, and it often dictates whether your message is opened and read. In fact, some studies report that 90% of the time the subject line alone

FIGURE 11.1: *A sample of an effective newsletter with all clickable content indicated by arrows. The email tracking software records reader interaction with these links, allowing you to identify leads and track reader engagement*

determines whether a recipient will read your message, so the importance of how you phrase the subject cannot be overestimated.

In general, the subject line should be long enough to explain the purpose of the email but also short enough for the reader to grasp the purpose quickly—and its content must be stated in a simple and straightforward manner. Also remember that different investors have different degrees of scientific sophistication. You cannot approach a private equity investor specialized in oncology in the same way as you would a philanthropically minded family office. Both the subject line and message must be thought-fully tailored for each destination.

Email campaigns conducted to set up meetings for a road trip receive the highest open and response rates when the subject line conveys to the potential investor exactly what the sender needs. This direct approach cuts through the "noise" of all the other communication in the investor's inbox. So begin the email by filling the subject line with the purpose of your message: "Meeting Request."

Next, give the prospect whom you are contacting a little context—tell him or her who you are. One option is to use your title and the name of your firm: "Meeting Request—Manager of XYZ Inc." Another option is to use a manager's name to give the email a personal touch: "Meeting Request—John Smith, Manager of XYZ Inc." You can adjust the style and format to your liking, but always be experimenting to find a subject line that gets the highest response rate.

Note the use of dashes in the subject lines above. Spacing characters such as these can help potential investors quickly scan the email header and decide whether they want to read it. A subject line that is easy to scan gives your email a chance to be considered. If your subject line contains a lot of information that is difficult to digest, investors will usually hit the delete button. So after stating the purpose of your email, use a spacing character for ease of reading.

Complete the heading with the final details of the marketing trip—the location and date. An option is to keep it geographically broad: "Meeting Request—Manager of XYZ Inc., California Trip, July 7–12," and then create your itinerary according to the investor interest you receive. Or you could mention the cities specifically: "Meeting Request—Manager of XYZ Inc., Trip to LA and SF Bay area, July 7–12."

In some cases, you may want to purposely keep the location broad—even if you don't have the flexibility to visit other cities. The reason is simple: the wider the area you provide in the subject line, the higher the response rate. You want to establish relationships with as many prospects as possible, so target as broad an area as is reasonable. Once you begin to dialogue with a potential investor, you can clarify the exact cities you will be visiting; perhaps the investor will be willing to travel to see you. Or if this prospect is particularly promising, you might decide to make a special arrangement to visit them. Either way, you have made contact and begun a dialogue.

Email campaigns for marketing trips usually benefit from multiple attempts to reach prospects. It is important that subsequent attempts be reflected in the subject line. In many cases, your original email message never reached its target, was deleted before it was reviewed, or simply got lost in cyberspace. Given the large amount of email communication received by prospects, you can assume that about half of the recipients never saw your original email or didn't recognize who it was from. So it is a best practice to attempt a second email campaign to your target audience after removing those who responded to your original email.

In many cases, a second email attempt can have a higher response rate than the original email. The primary reason for this rests in the wording of the subject line. At the very start of the subject line, include the words "2nd Attempt." Follow this with the original email heading, for example, "2nd Attempt—Meeting Request—Manager of XYZ Inc., California Trip, July 7–12." By making recipients aware that you have tried to reach them previously, they are more likely to review your email.

Finally, as you approach the date of your marketing trip, you may have meeting slots open and prospective investors you have not heard from. A different email technique can be applied here. This type of email usually is shorter than your original one. The purpose of the truncated format is to express a sense of informality and to convey that on the eve of the trip, you are dashing off an invitation for a last-minute meeting. The informality of the email, along with the quickly approaching date, usually results in higher response rates from prospects who are motivated by the deadline.

Composing the right subject line is the key to using this technique effectively. Instead of the more formal "Meeting Request," it should read as a short note to a colleague, for example, "Possible meeting next week in LA?" Note that you want to be specific with the location in this type of email. You can also use this type of email during the trip to fill in any remaining slots. Simply change "next week" to "this week." The informal style and short time frame usually result in shaking a few leads free.

The Body

After constructing a compelling subject that gets prospects' attention, you need to write a message that holds their interest and results in action. The trick is to adequately explain your purpose for contacting them without making the message too long. Over the following pages I am going to focus on general email marketing campaigns rather than specific correspondence to prospects with whom you are already communicating.

To construct an email message that results in a dialogue with a prospect, it is best to divide the content into short, concise paragraphs. Ideally, you want the body of the email to display directly on the screen when your recipient opens it. At most, the recipient should have to scroll down once if he or she is using a compressed reading pane. Aim for two to four paragraphs, each comprising two to four sentences that explain who, what, when, where, and how. Remember that these points should be tailored specifically to each investor category, as scientific literacy is variable among different types of investors.

The first paragraph is your introduction. It should explain why you are reaching out and offer your prospect a reason to continue reading. If you want to schedule a meeting, you may want to introduce your firm, and say what you do: "I hope this email finds you well. I am a partner at XYZ Inc. I will be traveling to London next week and I wanted to see if a meeting makes sense." If you have never met before, sometimes it helps to say that you don't believe the recipient has been introduced to your firm or has worked with your firm in the past.

If the email is an announcement, in addition to explaining why you are reaching out, you should also summarize the (hopefully positive) news. Again, should the recipient have a small reading pane that only displays a few sentences, you want to make sure that you are clear, concise, and compelling so he or she can get the gist of your communication and be intrigued enough to read further.

The few short paragraphs following the introduction should explain your purpose in a bit more detail. The ultimate goal is to get your prospect to act, so the body of the email is simply a tool used to create communication. Many fundraisers fail in this respect. They think they need to put all their cards on the table and include a lot of details. Or they believe that prospective investors only want laboratory research or trial data. As a result, their communiqués are long and wordy or read like an annual audit statement, which only encourages the prospect to click the "delete" button.

Remember, your prospects are human and thus the common metrics of marketing apply: you have only a few seconds, assuming that your prospects have decided to read your email, to capture their interest, convey your purpose, and get them to act. You need to be concise. If you get to the point, state it clearly, and back it up with key data points, your email will have a better chance of cutting through the clutter and noise, grabbing the prospects' attention, and getting them to act.

You may wonder how to craft a message to prospects with whom you have spoken in the past but are not in active communication. If it has been six months or more since you last spoke with them, it is probably a good idea to refresh their memory on your firm's product. Never assume that a prospect knows or remembers you; when in doubt, always err on the side of re-introducing your firm and putting a potential investor in context with what you are doing today.

The tone of these emails should also be more conversational than that used in an email blast. The point is to engage your contact in a more informal manner, as if to pick up where you left off in your last conversation. To use the road-show example, you could first begin by stating the topic of the email and why you are reaching out: "I am going to be back in San Francisco next week. When we last met nine months ago, you stated your firm was not yet ready for an offering like ours. I wanted to circle back to meet and give you an update on my firm."

Before distributing an email to prospects, many marketers often feel compelled to include an attachment—sometimes many. There is a common misunderstanding that more is better. However, for an introductory email, it is usually best to limit the number of attachments—perhaps a one- or two-page firm overview or the most recent commentary on your firm. Remember your goal and avoid the temptation to overwhelm your prospects with data. Email campaigns are meant to whet a prospect's appetite, not answer every possible question he or she might have (see Figure 11.2)

From: ▓▓▓▓▓▓▓▓▓▓▓▓▓▓▓▓▓▓▓▓▓▓▓▓
Sent: Tuesday, October 30, 2012 10:31 AM
To: ▓▓▓▓▓▓@lifesciencenation.com
Subject: Non-Toxic Cancer Drug Presents Dramatic Pre-Clinical Results

Dear ▓▓▓▓▓,

My name is ▓▓▓▓▓▓▓▓▓▓. I am the CEO of ▓▓▓▓▓▓▓▓▓. I write this email in the hope of arranging an introductory call. I have done some research on your firm and believe it might be worthwhile for us to speak.

▓▓▓▓▓▓▓▓. is based in Boston, MA and was founded by ▓▓▓▓▓▓▓▓▓▓▓▓▓▓▓▓▓▓ ▓▓▓▓▓▓▓▓▓▓▓▓▓▓▓▓▓▓▓▓▓▓▓▓▓▓▓ and myself. Our science is based on their groundbreaking investigations in chemistry and cellular biophysics.

Our Lead Product, ▓▓▓▓▓▓ is a novel, effective anti-cancer drug which has completed phase 1A clinical study. Unlike existing cancer therapies, ▓▓▓▓▓▓ has proven to be safe and non-toxic. In animal tests, ▓▓▓▓▓▓, either alone or in combination with chemotherapy drugs, eradicates a wide range of cancerous tumors and metastases. ▓▓▓▓▓▓ is inexpensive and simple to manufacture and can be administered either orally or intravenously. It can be used alone or in conjunction with radiation or chemotherapy to dramatically increase efficacy and reduce toxicity.

▓▓▓▓▓▓ has secured FDA Approval to conduct the next phase of clinical trials in order to demonstrate the drug's efficacy in cancer patients. We expect our clinical trials on cancer patients to begin within the next several months in ▓▓▓▓▓▓.

I would be happy to continue the conversation if you are interested in learning more about our company. I will have my administrative assistant reach out to you to set up a short introductory phone call.

Best,

▓▓▓▓▓▓

FIGURE 11.2: *Example of an effective introductory email. It clearly and succinctly explains intent and puts the reader in context without any superfluous information.*

Follow-Up Meetings and Task Management

At this point you are probably feeling overwhelmed by the amount of investors with whom you need to follow up, in addition to the task of keeping all the notes outlining the next step for each investor conversation you have had.

Unsophisticated fundraising executives make the mistake of using Excel to keep track of all this information. Using Excel usually results in a multicolored spreadsheet with 30 columns and hundreds of rows. As you can imagine, this process quickly becomes unmanageable, leading to confusion and frustration. To manage your information, you should use a cloud-based application such as Salesforce or ACT. Salesforce (which was recommended in Chapter 8) is a task and list management system (TLMS) that will allow you to create your own custom profile and enable you to jot down notes and keep track of where you are in the dialogue process with each investor. These applications are accessible through the cloud and serve as a repository for all your contacts and communications. Next is an example of a profile on Salesforce.com (Figure 11.3).

As you design your custom profile, you will want to be sure to include the following important fields:

- **Next Activity:** Notifies me of the next time I need to follow up with the investor
- **Last Email:** Notifies me of the last time I sent the investor an email
- **Description:** Shows me a brief description of the investor and his or her investment interests
- **Notes:** Enables me to quickly jot down notes regarding the next step in the investment process
- **Status of Lead:** Allows me to classify investors based on interest, providing me with the ability to self-filter investors once a dialogue has been initiated

Summary

The successful execution of an email campaign is both a science and an art. Honing the process requires time and experimentation, and it is a constant work in progress. Listen to your audience! Clicks and opens are one of the best indicators of interest in your content, and by monitoring what your audience opens and clicks over time, you can begin to change the overall message and tone of your mailings.

Most importantly, the initial email is only the beginning of the long and more challenging follow-up process of maintaining a relationship. What this means for you, the fundraising executive, is that you have to be *diligent*. It takes 10 to 15 calls to get someone whom you have not met on the phone to start a dialogue.

Sample Investor

salesforce.com

▶ Owner Info

▼ Status

Next Follow up Date	5/8/2014
Date of Last Email	1/1/2014
Status of Lead	In Play
Date of Last Voicemail	1/1/2014

▼ Account Information

Account Name	Sample Investor [View Hierarchy]
Company Type	
Website	http://www.sampleinvestor.com
Phone	111-111-1111

▼ Description Information

Description	Sample Investor is a family office based in New York City. The family office controls approximately $500 million in assets. $50 million of this is dedicated to advancing oncology research via direct investment in therapeutic companies. The motivation for this is a prevalence of breast cancer in the family.
Billing Address	123 Sample Street New York City, NY 11111 USA

▼ Notes

Notes	Met at event in late December 2013. Very interested.
Rep Name	
Status of Lead (Sales)	
Sales Notes	

FIGURE 11.3: *Sample profile on Salesforce.com*

Once you finally make contact and begin that dialogue, it can take another 7 to 10 phone calls just to reconnect. After all that, if you manage to create a relationship and know someone fairly well, it can take 5 to 7 attempts to get that person on the phone. The most surprising statistic may be that most people give up after the first 3 or 4 attempts. You must be persistent and tenacious, and whatever you do, *don't give up*. Your tenacity will impress investors, as it will speak to your commitment to advance your company to the next level. With dogged determination, a carefully planned email campaign targeting a group of investors that are the right fit for you, and a little bit of luck, you'll be well on your way toward closing your next round of capital.

Understanding the Fundraising Process

CHAPTER 12

Anatomy of an Allocation Process

Every allocation process is different, but they all generally follow a similar timeline and involve people functioning in the same roles. In order to map out this process, I created a graphic that lays out the path toward allocation (see Figure 12.1). Hopefully this will help you get your bearings in any deal in which you are involved and identify in which stage of the process you are and for what next step you need to prepare. Additionally, as you begin to reach out and speak with potential investors, it can be helpful to understand the role of those with whom you are dialoguing.

To help you map out the individuals taking part in the allocation process, I refer to six different roles: information gatherers, gatekeepers, evaluators, navigators, recommenders, and decision makers. Keep in mind that these roles aren't always filled by different individuals. Sometimes one person can embody all of them, or sometimes a group of people serve the function of one or more of them. In whatever form they take, it will help you immensely to try and identify what "character" or combination of characters you are encountering at each step of the process.

In previous chapters, we've talked about finding potential investors so you can begin to build relationships that eventually lead to investment. The life

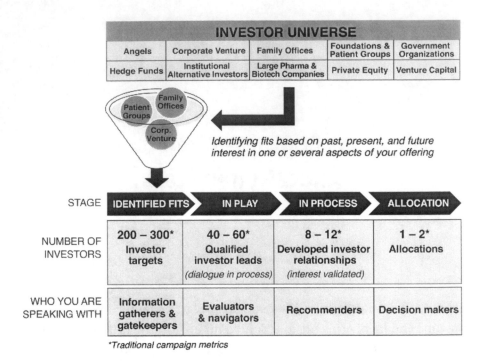

FIGURE 12.1: *Anatomy of an allocation process*

science arena is full of potential investors: Life Science Nation (LSN) has identified 10 categories of life science investors and about 5,000 institutional organizations, private firms, and nonprofits that allocate to the life sciences. Your job is to ferret out targets based on your firm's investor profile, evaluate their viability as investors for you, and then get them on or off your plate as fast as possible. A good target is one that has a chance of being a fit.

To review, a fit is when a prospect has a real need for your company's products or service, has decided on a specific investment strategy, and has a mandate to make the allocation. If a target passes this initial qualification test, it becomes a prospect. It becomes a *hot* prospect when the allocation time frame is relevant to your current fundraising goals.

Keep in mind that the typical allocation time frame is 9 to 12 months or more. This gives an investor time to extensively research the management team and watch how a company works for two or three quarters before investing. Like you, the fundraising executive, the investor also has to find a fit for his or her mandate, validate the fit, vet the technology, find and vet your competitors, establish a working relationship with you, observe how you and your management team interact both internally as a firm and externally as an investment prospect, perform due diligence, and conduct all the other time-consuming business required to make an allocation. This cannot take place overnight, and it must begin with identifying a fit.

Identification

The first stage of the allocation process is what I call the "identification stage." It's the phase when you make contact with a target investor, they express an interest, and you officially identify them as a prospect. This is when you have a meeting or two and a dialogue begins. When you have a prospect, you are in the game and playing for money, although at this stage, your chances of turning a prospect into an investor are only 10%. You are at the beginning of the pipeline, or "the pipe," as I like to call it.

The pipe is a way to measure the progress of allocation processes. It's the antidote to fruitless meetings and a strategy of hoping and wishing. If your company doesn't have a way to classify the status of your prospects, do whatever it takes to implement a system that can be used by everyone in your company who is participating in the fundraising process and ensure they adhere to it. Get yourself and the executives in the same room. Start a dialogue. Outline what it takes to get an allocation. Have the team and the powers that be sign on and agree that this will be the new process of raising cash.

When you're in the identification stage, you're likely talking or meeting with the "information gatherers" or the "gatekeepers." These two groups are part of the investor landscape, and after talking with these people you'll get a sense of whether you are a fit for a potential investment. However, you don't want to put a potential investor in the firm's pipeline until you have met with the "navigators" and "decision makers" (later in the process) and feel positive about the fit. It's imperative to begin outreach with many prospects all the time; don't forget that this is a numbers game.

The Information Gatherers

Usually, the information gatherers are folks who are good at ferreting out information and understanding a firm's products and services. They don't necessarily know all the specifics, such as why they have been assigned a task, what the information they uncover will be used for, or when that information will be used. They may not be able to answer in-depth questions regarding specific details of the investment mandate, because they often have a limited scope of the company. All they know is that they've been asked to use their analytical brains to gather and collect information on certain types of firms and their technologies.

Sometimes life science fundraising executives think of a meeting with an information gatherer as more important or pivotal than it is. Recognize this kind of meeting as a simple informational transaction—that's what it is. Provide the information in as nice a package as you can, and then go on your merry way. Investors do not automatically become hot prospects when you hand them some information. Remember that winning an allocation is a long process, and you've just taken the first step on that road.

Having said that, you can't take anything for granted. In your initial meeting or conversation, you must probe to make sure the information gatherer really is in a low-level position and not more powerful than that. I remember a conversation I once had with an information gatherer when I was an executive at a software technology company. I asked him what he was looking to do.

"Who, me? I'm just collecting some data on some stuff we're looking at."

"What stuff?" I asked.

"Oh, I'm trying to understand what companies are doing in this area and the products they have. Then I'll pass the info along to some folks in the company."

"What for?"

"We're trying to make some decisions, I guess."

"Well, who are you and what do you do?"

"Who, me? Oh! I'm the CTO of IBM's Life Sciences Group."

Bingo!

Keep in mind that the answer could have been that he was a student doing an internship. In fact, most information gatherers are not key players. A CEO asks the SVP to identify the top ten vendors that market a specific product. The SVP delegates the task to the VP, who gives it to a department manager, who assigns it to an associate, who passes it on to an assistant, who gives it to the intern. That's a common pathway in a typical corporate structure.

However, sometimes CEOs and other top-level executives are in a hurry and don't want to wait around for the information. They may decide that they can do a Google search as quickly as the next guy and line up a couple of meetings. So always find out who you are speaking with and why. You never know at which stage you will meet the right person!

Open Sesame—the Gatekeepers

The gatekeepers keep you out or let you in. Most accomplish this task by ensuring that all inquiries for investment lead to them. They tell the receptionists, administrators, and everyone else in their company to "send them unto me."

Let's say you are calling an executive level player, and you get through— you get the managing partner on the line. They might refer you down the ladder to somebody, or days later, someone else might call you back. This person is usually the gatekeeper. Maybe the investor is looking for an emerging therapeutics company and is not interested in medical devices. In this case the gatekeeper would be tasked with only allowing the emerging therapeutics companies to initiate a dialogue.

The gatekeeper is probably the first stop for your emails, phone calls, and slide deck. This person is in the know regarding exactly what relationships the company is interested in; part of the gatekeeper's job description is to bring opportunities into the firm and turn away nuisances. For the most part, gatekeepers are easy to find, as they tend to be in the "front of the house" or within arm's reach of the executive suite. They usually are knowledgeable about the firm. They will likely usher you in if you have something that makes sense, but they do not suffer fools gladly.

The gatekeepers are incredibly busy folks who are besieged by life science fundraising executives, so it's hard to get their attention. In the life science investment arena, there are about 15,000 start-ups trying to catch the interest of approximately 5,000 investors. As a result, gatekeepers are inundated with hundreds of emails, phone calls, and slide decks in a typical week. That's a lot of day-to-day noise. To stand out, your best bet is to send the gatekeepers some crisp, timely information that you know they need. Of course, to know what they need, you have to do your homework. These are binary folks. They are more impressed with solid, concise bottom-line rationales than glad-handing and aggressive salesmanship (although it never hurts to be friendly and personable in your delivery).

The gatekeepers are not going to give you a lot of opportunities to get past them. Your first attempt must be well thought-out and well planned, and you must be organized. Before you contact them, for example, have an email package ready to send as soon as you get off the phone. Before you meet with them, make sure you know everything about your company and theirs. If you don't, bring someone with you who does. If you tell a gate-keeper that you want to bring one of your colleagues along to talk to him or her personally, he or she might volunteer to invite some other folks in his or her firm as well—or not. If not, then you know this gatekeeper has clout.

No matter what, it is imperative to get a meeting scheduled with these people. Utilize the gatekeeper to map the firm's players and learn about the company's process. Of course, you should create your own map first.

Mapping a Company

There are various ways to map firms that make life science investments (see Figure 12.2). At one extreme are the life science fundraising executives who approach the task as if it were a reconnaissance mission. They gather all the information they can find and comb through it before the big meeting. They conduct an exhaustive analysis of the prospect and its peers (other possible leads), as well as the industry. At the other extreme are those who do just enough research to have a good idea of the

Mapping a Company

Platform	Personnel/Information to Search For
Company Website	Management team, board of directors, press releases, portfolio announcements
Google, Yahoo!, Bing	CEO, management team, portfolio information *Hint: Search for "company name + last year's date (e.g., 2013)" and another search for "company name + this year's date (e.g., 2014)"*
LinkedIn	Bios of CEO and management team, 1st-degree and 2nd-degree connections with folks inside the company, groups that the team members have joined, recent visits
CrunchBase	Management team, portfolio companies, and a gauge of the company's investment activity
ZoomInfo	Direct phone number and email address
Popular News Sites (e.g., Fierce Biotech)	Context regarding the firm's current and future plans and a gauge of public opinion
Conferences	Speakers, attendees, and partnering opportunities
LSN Company & Investor Databases	Allocation information, sectors and subsectors of interest, company and management team preferences, message from the investor

FIGURE 12.2: *Information to uncover and some suggested resources to use when mapping a company*

prospect's specific investment category and gather the rest through real-time, face-to-face dialogue.

There are many pros and cons to these two methods, and either one or a combination thereof will probably fit you. One advantage to the deep-dive investigative approach is that prospects perceive you as well informed, credible, and perceptive. This evokes respect and trust, which help you forge solid relationships. However, I've seen life science fundraising executives who spend way too much time researching and not nearly enough on the phone or on the road. And when they finally do talk with a prospect, they are so focused on verifying their data that they don't really hear what the prospect is saying.

Now, don't get me wrong. You must verify your data. Some life science fundraising executives simply assume that the information they gathered up front is correct. They don't confirm it, and they pay the price later on. There are also those who believe themselves to be faster on their feet than they really are, and they mistake "less prep" for "no prep," leading to disastrous results. It's hard to gauge how much up-front time you should spend on research, but successful life science fundraising executives find a happy middle ground between these two extremes.

Regardless of the approach you take, it is vital that you listen holistically when meeting with prospects. You must draw people out, read between the lines, verify what you hear, connect the dots, and ask and answer questions. An honest, real-time dialogue fosters respect and trust and lays the foundation of a good relationship. It also makes the most of the time you will be spending in contact with prospects.

First Impressions

So you are meeting the information gatherer or gatekeeper and starting a dialogue. This is a critical point. During the first few meetings, prospects form an impression of you and your company that sticks with them and becomes their long-term view. Avoid getting too aggressive when you are in sales mode. During a meeting, you should confirm your map of the company, verify that there is a mandate and timeline, establish an outline of the allocation process, discover a few pain points, find out if they're talking to your competitors, and zero in on who will be the ultimate navigator of the process. This is your opportunity to draw the prospect out, open up a dialogue, and have an honest exchange of information, and it is the time when everyone gets comfortable.

Your mind-set when it comes to your approach can be critical in fostering positive first impressions. Every time you call on a prospect—whether it's an information gatherer, gatekeeper, or even a decision maker—think of your goal as to get to know a new person, not secure an allocation. Imagine that you are meeting a new friend who is interested in your work.

When I go into meetings, I want prospects to form the impression that my team and I are professional, prepared, and know what we're doing. At the end, I want prospects to thank me for an informative meeting and hear the words "we look forward to working with you." I also want to be able to say the same thing in return.

It's Only the Beginning

During the identification stage, the puzzle pieces of the deal start to fit together, a relationship forms, and the allocation process seems to be off to a great start. Unfortunately, this is also where many life science fundraising executives are led astray by seeing an allocation where there really isn't or shouldn't be one.

Let's face it: life science fundraising executives feel pressure to put something on their forecast. Because they are anxious to turn a target into a prospect, they often begin to see things that aren't there, try to force a fit, or use every skill they have to push along a relationship that they shouldn't. Don't fall into this trap!

Listen to your gut. Think back to an allocation process that came together as it should have. Remember the circumstances that gave you confidence, and the moment you knew you could honestly say to yourself, "They will be an investor. They just don't know it yet." Then stay in the real world. Opportunities can change direction, be postponed, stumble and fall off a cliff, and flat-out die. They are very tricky creatures. They prey upon your optimistic nature. They get you in a fix.

That is why it's imperative to concentrate on the prospects who are a fit and move on from investors who aren't, pronto! It is also the reason to set everyone's expectations at the outset of the process. Let those in your company know that a potential client is ready for the forecast list only when you've made it halfway through the allocation process with them. A forecast list is composed of investors you have qualified who have also qualified your firm and who may give you money.

Movin' Down the Pipe—In Play

After initially qualifying a prospect, the next step is to develop a relationship. You must recognize that this takes time, so don't rush, overwhelm, or hassle the prospect, no matter how much pressure to fundraise is being exerted on you internally or externally. The allocation process takes time; in fact, the timeline is longer than it used to be. The process spans, at a minimum, 9 to 12 months and can easily get stretched out further. That is why it's important to have many irons in the fire. You'll make very little progress if all you do is worry about and bother a few prospects. You must cast a wide net and then learn to relax, give your prospects some time, and avoid overwhelming them with your overzealous desire to get an allocation.

Don't smother or tick off a prospect because you have ants in your pants. Take the time to develop relationships with the right folks. The right individuals to contact at this stage are the "evaluators," the "navigators," and the "recommenders."

The Evaluators

When the evaluators enter the picture, the game is afoot! The evaluators are the people who roll up their sleeves and look closely at your firm over the long term. This means they listen to your pitch, meet your company's founders and executive team, and then monitor your firm's progress from quarter to quarter. To stay on their radar screens, you have to come up with ways of communicating that are nonintrusive but allow you to maintain a relationship. It might be via white papers, emails, newsletters, or conference calls, but you must find some way to keep them abreast of your company's ongoing progress.

The evaluators also watch to see how your firm's executives react when they meet or beat their predictions and how they act when they miss. This behavior is at the forefront of investors' minds today, because it lets them know how your business functions in coping with the ups and downs of the real world. The new modus operandi of investors is to watch and wait, validate performance and milestone achievement, and get to know the executive team. "Relationships" and "transparency" are the new buzz words. You and your firm need to be ready with cogent answers and commentary through the good times and bad so prospects can see what kind of long-term relationship they might be entering into.

It is easy to make a good impression on evaluators and just as easy to foul up a relationship with them. I have seen countless life science fundraising executives make the mistake of delegating the due diligence process to some-body else within their firm, instead of being present at all meetings. However, strange things can happen. What you thought would be a slam-dunk evalu-ation can turn into a full-blown firestorm over the most inane and innocuous details. A run-of-the-mill meeting can suddenly be dominated by people who love to one-up each other by showing how smart or knowledgeable they are regarding a technology or the current and future state of the market.

You must be ever vigilant during this process and leave absolutely noth-ing to chance. If the sparks start to fly, you have to be there to put out the fire and calm the group. The best way to start a meeting is to go over the agenda for it, making sure everyone is on the same page and knows why they are there. Then set the stage by providing the context for the product and market. Keep it simple.

Part of your agenda should be to present your firm and highlight the synergies between it and the investor's mandate. Be wary of allowing folks to take each other down rat holes. It happens all the time: two people go off topic and head straight into never-never land. You must always keep the group focused and avoid getting involved in the chase.

As you explain your firm's strategy, your understanding of the investor's mandate, and how you may fulfill their requirements, you should be getting some sort of positive feedback from your audience. They may be smiling, voicing their agreement, or simply nodding—all good signs. If there's dis-agreement, smirks, or scowls—or worse, no reaction whatsoever—you are in trouble. Take action fast.

Start with some open questions, such as "Mr. Evaluator, are we showing you what you want to see? Did you expect something else? Did we misun-derstand what you are looking for or what your needs are? I'm sensing a potential disconnect here. Are we disconnecting?"

Such direct, open questions should elicit some feedback. Then you can adjust or regroup. Never let a meeting deteriorate without trying to understand why: "Mr. Evaluator, I feel we are heading south here. Please tell me why."

One all-too-common occurrence after company and technology presentations is the shoulda-woulda-coulda phenomenon. Your team is in the car, in the restaurant, or back at the office after an investor presentation. One by one, the members start to dissect the meeting and the reaction of the participants: "Do you think the investor understood our new product and technology?" "Do you think he doubted our time to market numbers?" "Do we know when and how the firm is planning to make the allocation?"

These are all good questions THAT SHOULD HAVE BEEN ASKED DURING THE MEETING.

Do not waste a meeting with an investor prospect. If you have thoughts, questions, observations, or insights, speak up! The meeting is the time for that, while you're all together. Get it all out on the table. Point out any issues you perceive on their side or yours and get them resolved. Otherwise you will be forced to go into catch-up mode: asking for another meeting so you can address some open issues or tracking down the participants individually to clear things up. This is frustrating and time consuming, and though sometimes it will be necessary, it can usually be avoided.

Don't forget that in-person meetings are vital. No one is going to make an investment in a firm without evaluating the science and the team. Unfortunately there is a lot of misinformation circulating from so-called experts who either haven't raised money in a long time or have never raised money before. This has led some life science fundraising executives to believe that they can get around the long due diligence process. They believe that meeting after meeting slows down the process and that allocations could be made much more quickly if that step was eliminated.

However, ongoing meetings are probably the most important part of the allocation process. They provide the investor with a hands-on look at your firm's technology and an understanding of the management team.

The Navigators

At some point, as an allocation process progresses through the pipe, the navigator surfaces. The navigator usually appears during the in-play stage, and the person filling this role has the most at stake. This individual's success is riding on the outcome of the allocation process—whether that allocation is given to you or your competitor.

The navigator will usually come to you and has knowledge of how to guide you through his or her world, which is the particular investor firm with whom he or she works. The navigator may be in the room with the evaluators and might even be an evaluator. Or he or she may surface in some other way. If the navigator doesn't surface, you must find someone with whom you are interacting that can function in this role for you. You need someone who can be a behind-the-scenes ally.

The navigator is your go-to guy or gal, your sponsor, your new best friend, and the person you need to convince. Correctly identifying the navigator is imperative. It is also tricky, as many people you meet along the way will lead you to believe that they are the navigator. But actions speak louder than words, and you have to figure out who the real navigator is—the one who's going to guide you through to the end. This is one of the reasons why I mentioned earlier that you should always verify with whom you're speaking. Miss the navigator and you may miss your allocation.

The Due Diligence Process

It is rare for investors to choose a life science firm in a vacuum. Rather, they conduct a search, winnow their options down to a short list, and then begin the due diligence process. Though technically due diligence starts with the first meeting, investors generally don't spend the time and resources required for it unless they are seriously considering investing in a firm. Therefore, the formalized aspect of due diligence is usually conducted toward the end of the allocation process and comprises many aspects of the final vetting of the team, company, and product.

Investors today approach the due diligence process with more seriousness than they did in the past, and the group of new investors on the scene is equipped with a series of best practices. Family offices and other small investors are now adopting the due diligence practices of large investors, such as private equity funds and VCs. And large investors are reevaluating their processes to ensure they are rigorous enough, often adding new procedures, such as background checks on management personnel.

This focus on research is the main reason that the due diligence process takes longer than it once did. Combine this with the fact that investors want to monitor the clinical path closely, develop a relationship with the executive team, and get to know the CEO, and it's no wonder that what used to take as few as 6 months may now require as many as 12 or more.

So what does the due diligence process entail? Any good investor will explain how he or she will go about doing due diligence on you, your firm, and your product. Throughout the allocation process you will want to keep your attorney apprised of events so he or she can guide the process and make sure that you are on the right side of any issues that may arise. There's no doubt that due diligence is a laborious process, but it is a must. Throughout this book, we have talked about putting your best foot forward. Think of the due diligence process as another opportunity to do just that.

Most investors will make multiple visits to your firm. So be prepared, should an investor request multiple meetings. Often they will ask for a meeting that focuses on the "going forward process"; they will use this to get on the same page with you regarding timelines and directions of the product investment. The investors want to make sure that all your in-house and outsourced resources can support their idea of how to move the product forward. They'll want check that the overall operations pass muster. The best thing you can do during on-site visits is be as open and accommodating as possible with potential investors. These meetings are the first steps toward building trust.

No matter how thorough the on-site visits are, you should anticipate follow-up questions. In fact, it is highly likely that you will receive a request for some bit of information that you do not have at your fingertips. Your best bet is to find it, and find it fast. Sometimes such requests are being made as tests. Investors often want to see how organized you are and how quickly you can react. If you want to stay in the race, get on it.

After all your information is in the hands of a potential investor, there is not much else to do, which is why we have a saying at LSN that "companies are bought rather than sold." Ultimately, investors are trying to position your firm and others within their portfolios. They have constructed those portfolios based on their own particular outlook and set of assumptions, and they have certain expectations of how their investments should perform in various market conditions. So after all the questions are asked and answered, investors will sit down and evaluate how your firm fits within the specific scenarios they have in mind.

Some life science fundraising executives have the misconception that investors "shop" for firms to invest in, but nothing could be further from the truth. Most investors understand that life science companies are complex and nuanced and dependent upon experimental science. Trying to compare them is like trying to compare apples to oranges. Investors create mandates for their investments and then carry out the mandates as best as they can.

The Midpoint

When your allocation process reaches the middle of the in-play stage, you have something that is alive and kicking. Another way of looking at it is that the allocation is "yours to lose." At this stage, you are fully engaged and are halfway down the path toward getting an allocation. The discussions and information exchanges are in full swing. The relationship and dialogue are good. You've teamed up with the right people. It is truly a great feeling when your phone is ringing with questions and your calls are being returned.

The Value Propositions

As a life science fundraising executive, you are continually conveying the value proposition of your firm. But as you head into the midway point of the allocation process, you need to be absolutely sure that the potential investor understands your value propositions and maybe even has brought some of his or her own to your attention. When a prospect sees the value in your company, wants your product, and knows why it's a good thing, you will be well on your way to winning an allocation.

It is precisely at this point that you must avoid falling all over yourself trying to get the allocation locked in. You must make sure that the prospect truly understands the value in your company and that he or she is convinced your firm is a fit. If you try to close an allocation when the value propositions are not fully understood, you decrease your chances of success. Don't assume a potential investor truly understands the value simply because he or she says so. Verify it by saying, "So, Mr. Prospect, it seems that you see the value of my firm and that it is a fit for you. Please take a moment and explain to me what you've learned and why it works for you and your current mandate. It would help me to hear it from your perspective."

You will likely get one of three responses:

- The prospect may echo the value propositions you have conveyed. If this happens, bravo! You've done well.

- The prospect may cite one or more value propositions that you've never heard before. This is also good. The fact is that it does not matter what you think the value propositions are. Your prospect knows what they are for him or her, so listen closely. He or she is giving you a gift: new value propositions that you can use to pitch other prospects.

- The prospect may be unable to articulate any value propositions. In this case, either he or she doesn't really understand what the value propositions are or you missed something along the way. This indicates that you must go back to square one. Start the marketing process over, right from the get-go. Take the prospect on the journey that you thought got you to fifty-fifty. Pull up a chair, cancel all your calls, get some coffee, and begin: "So, we started talking to you folks about three months ago . . ."

At this point in the allocation process, most investors have a short list of firms they have vetted and will next home in on the managers to determine who is most competent and offers the most favorable opportunity for making returns on their investment. Usually this means that the recommender or decision maker is courting a few managers. Remember that talking to an investment executive and being told that you may receive the allocation isn't the final step in the process. The allocation isn't even officially yours when the decision maker or one of the executive players says directly, "Joe, you and your firm have been chosen for an allocation." However, this is known as a "verbal," and receiving it means that you are actually close to sealing the deal.

A verbal is a milestone in the allocation process, but it is not a signed document; at this point it is important to remember that you do not have a check cashed and money in your bank account. A verbal is great, but it also means you need to be really attentive in order to move forward and receive a signed contract. I have received many verbals in my business development life that did not culminate for one reason or another in an allocation; that is part of the reality of making deals. Remember that they are never done until they are done!

The Recommenders

The recommenders are pivotal to the process—their opinions and recommendations really count. They generally stay behind the scenes until after a firm has moved from the in-play stage to the in-process one. Recommenders base their referral on the information gathered by the information gatherers, gatekeepers, and evaluators, and they are the ones who consolidate all of it into a solid, concise package to send on to the decision maker.

If you impress the recommender, you have a good shot at winning the allocation. When you meet with him or her, you will start talking more seriously and specifically about time to market and market size. The recommender will narrow his or her choices down to a handful of firms, and you can safely assume that all your competitors will still be in the running. Whoever has the most impressive fundraising executive, management team, and products and service will be recommended to the decision maker.

To be successful, you must work on developing good relationships with *all* the people involved in the investment process: those within your own company and those at the investor's. But you must especially make an effort with the recommender. The better the relationship, the easier it is to stay up to date on any new issues that crop up (and they will—wrinkles never stop presenting themselves in this process) and figure out how to address them.

Always keep in mind this simple fact: an allocation process starts out with a particular mandate, which is defined by a set of requirements. You have to understand the mandate requirements and keep your eye on what is happening during the evaluation process. The fundraising executive who stays on top of each subtle change of events that can affect the process usually wins because he or she is current and in context.

Timing Is Everything

Timing can be a blessing or a curse in every allocation process. The status of allocations often changes on a quarterly basis. Sometimes the process rolls over into the next quarter, and sometimes mandates dictate that it is completed. Often, the sense of timing and urgency depends on the people involved. A decision maker may want to complete an allocation process quickly, but the navigator or the recommender he or she has assigned to it may be overloaded and may not have the bandwidth to accomplish this.

Once you have received a verbal that your firm has been selected for the allocation, then you must wait for the agreement to show up, which could take weeks, months, a quarter, or longer, depending on many variables. Waiting to hear from investors can drive even the most patient executive close to the edge. Knowing the investment cycle of investors can save you much anxiety. For example, family offices generally have access to capital and, as a result, these firms are more opportunistic and make investments frequently. Pensions, endowments, and foundations, on the other hand, typically must have investments approved by a board of directors, which may meet only twice a year. They are not as nimble as family offices but make larger, longer-term allocations.

So get a handle on prospects' investment cycles. If you understand whether the wait is six weeks or six months, you'll sleep a lot better at night. You'll also be able to focus on pursuing other potential investors and keeping your pipeline full, which is really the key to securing allocations.

Allocation Phase

Raising capital in the life science arena is both a science and an art form. Yes, it requires professional collateral, a proactive marketing effort, and consistent follow-up. But because it hinges on building relationships, you also need to develop your intuition, a sixth sense for when to push and when to be patient. Perhaps nowhere in the process is this more evident than in the allocation phase.

The Decision Maker

Imagine that you've been courting an investor for months, maybe even for over a year. You suspect, or are told outright, that the odds are stacking up in your favor. You may have even received a verbal. You're anxious to see this come to fruition. Perhaps you're coming to the end of your fundraising cycle.

It's at this point that many life science fundraising executives have the inclination to push the process along, get the deal done, and get the term sheet signed. Usually, however, that's the worst thing you can do. Rather, you need to give the investor the time and space he or she needs to go through his or her process. Rarely is an investor acting alone, and the more people involved, the longer the process. So the best thing you can do is get an understanding of the players involved, the steps they need to take, and their timeline, and then get out of the way.

The decision maker is the person in the company who has the authority to write the check. This may be somebody you have met along the way a few times or someone who kept to themselves until the final week of the process. Either way, this is the person who will contact you at the end of the line and deliver a contract directly for you to sign. If you have made it all this way but another firm is chosen for the allocation, you may be contacted and hear a "no," but you may also hear nothing at all. This is another good reason to be diligent in your follow-up, so you can stay apprised of whether you are still in the running.

At the same time, there is no need to panic or waste any extra effort at this stage. In fact, it's better to move your sights and energy to another investor, for the more irons you have in the fire, the better. Before you move on, however, take time to think about how you got to this stage with this investor. What did the investor like or dislike about your firm? What questions were asked? Investors tend to think along similar lines, so it pays to incorporate what you learned from one process into the next one.

If you didn't receive the allocation, however, don't obsess about what may have gone wrong. It will drive you crazy. There are many aspects of this process that are not under your control. You must simply incorporate what you've learned into your approach and take comfort in the fact that you made it to the final round. Then stick the shovel in the ground and keep working.

CHAPTER 13

Straight Talk About Finding, Vetting, and Closing Capital

In concluding this book, there are a few important things I want to say about raising capital in general. Keep in mind that whether you like it or not, you have entered the world of sales, and you are tasked with selling yourself, your team, your firm, and your product to an investor. As I have stated throughout this book, outbound direct fundraising is a numbers game. Some 200 to 300 investor targets will net you 40 to 60 potential compelling fits with whom you will interact and thus create a dialogue. As you go through the relationship-building and vetting process, that list will likely be whittled down to 8 to 12 active potential clients. You can expect to have five or so in the final mix, which may result in one or two allocations of capital.

Starting a global outbound campaign to find capital takes time, dedication, commitment, and resources. You are not alone and more than likely face some stiff competition for those investment dollars. When you enter the arena, it's imperative to have clear expectations and understand the rules of the game. What follows are some kernels of advice gleaned from my many years of experience with this process.

Showcase Yourself—Get on the Road or on the Phone

As a life science fundraising executive, you must leave the building. The days of incoming inquiries are long gone. Figure out a way—any way—to get your feet on the road. You will never raise money by sitting around your office. You need to get in front of potential investors if you are going to market your product. Fundraising executives who spend more time in the office than they do at meetings will fail to reach their allocation potential. If this is you, you must regroup and get packing. There is no middle ground here. Once you have initiated the allocation process with several investors, you will need some in-office time—but not a lot. The allocation game is won in the field, through meeting with investors and developing solid long-term relationships.

I have a theory about successful life science fundraising executives: those who begin work first each day and quit last will generate the most allocation dollars. They rise early to create a daily schedule and make sure everything is prepared. Then they head out to the field or pick up the phone and spend the day in meetings or on calls, reserving time at the end of the day for follow-up. They usually work late, taking care of all action items, and then repeat the process the next day. This is how you achieve success in closing allocations.

At Life Science Nation (LSN), our salespeople engage in 30 to 40 calls, demos, or meetings with prospects a month, every month. Though meetings may not be occurring all the time, the sales team is working to secure those meetings every single day. Marketing is a full-time job that is as important as every other position at your firm. If you doubt this, your firm will be beaten by competitors who are beefing up their marketing efforts.

The Importance of Context

It is difficult to overstate the value of context. Context is basically the glue that holds the reality of a deal together on many levels. Keeping everyone in context means making sure that all the key players in your firm and all the key players on the other side of the table are on the same page and singing out of the same hymnal. This task is imperative; once people begin to get out of context, your deal is in jeopardy.

You know the moment: you're in a meeting trying to get a commitment that will move the process forward when someone pipes up and says, "I thought your product leapt tall buildings in a single bound." The scientist's eyes dart over to you and you say, "Well, not exactly, but it's faster than a speeding bullet."

Before the words are even out of your mouth, you know that was the wrong answer. But what's the right one? Who is that guy? And why do you get the distinct feeling that your allocation is suddenly on the ropes?

I'll tell you. During the allocation process, there are lots of meetings and many people moving in and out. It is hard to keep everyone on the same page, and this is the person that you missed. He has some wrong information. At this critical juncture, when you're looking to confirm that all is right with the world and the process, he's raising doubts.

Nothing can derail an allocation process faster than a prospect with the wrong information. It may be about your technology, your company, the time to market, their needs, their objectives, the fit, or any number of other things. It doesn't matter. The wrong information gets you off track.

This is why at the first appearance of a new individual you must rewind and start over. As soon as someone new comes into the room, deliver the summary of your presentation so far to him or her. When you move up a notch in the information exchange process, present your firm from scratch. At the moment when someone makes a statement or asks a question that could foul up the perception of your company or product, jump in with "Okay, Ms. Investor, let's take it from the top. Here's our expertise and new technology. These are the needs you have outlined in your mandate. Now, is that a fit?"

At every stage of the allocation process, you will meet people who will start brainstorming, think of what-if scenarios, or just go into fantasy overdrive. Don't let anyone derail the process. Put everyone in context. THIS MEANS EVERY SINGLE PERSON, EVERY SINGLE TIME.

This drudgery can drive a life science fundraising executive batty. It is tedious, repetitive, and difficult to accomplish. However, if you keep every sentient being who is involved in the allocation process on the same page, the process will go more smoothly and you will be in a better position than your competitors who don't worry about context. If you don't keep everyone in the loop, your prospects can miss important points about you, your company, and your product or service. The growing number of people involved in the allocation process, and the difficulty of keeping everyone in context, is one reason why it takes so long to get an allocation these days!

A typical context-setting session might progress like this:

- This is who we are as individuals and why we are here.
- This is who you are and what your current mandate is.
- This is our firm and technology and how it fits your mandate criteria.
- Here is the executive team's domain experience and years in the field.
- This is a summary of our last meeting. Do you agree?
- The goal of today's meeting is to keep moving toward a relationship.
- Here is the agenda for our meeting today. Is this correct?
- Here is what we hope to accomplish today and what we want to achieve tomorrow.
- If there's a fit, here is how things work in our company.
- If there's a fit, here's how we understand things work in your company.
- Here's where we're heading next.

This is a simple approach to getting everyone on the same page.

Keep in mind that you are marketing in a dynamic environment. People, specifications, requirements, the market, and many other things that affect the allocation process can change. Despite it all, you must keep everyone aware of and in agreement about the status. You must provide the context for participants in calls and meetings. Follow up with status reports to everyone. Do it constantly. This habit will serve you in the long run.

Fundraising Is Not for Wimps

Even if you do your job well, the allocation process will rarely be smooth. Be alert, be aware, and don't be afraid to make the tough calls. Allocation terms can change at any moment, teams can shift, the market can swing. Don't panic at each surprising turn of events. Under no circumstances should you get jumpy and start saying "yes" to things you should be saying "no" to. Always stay in control, and be clear-eyed and honest.

As you work with a prospect to understand the current mandate, rarely will you find it to be a perfect fit. You might be able to roll with some changes, by iterating your technology and pivoting your message. But if a mandate morphs and is no longer a fit for your firm, say so: "Mr. Investor, I've realized that my firm really isn't a fit for you. I appreciate the time you've spent with us. Here's the company to call. Ask for Bill. Tell him I suggested you call him. He can help you." Your good karma will be rewarded. Everyone appreciates a no-nonsense life science fundraising executive who doesn't waste time. Don't forge ahead and hope. Face the facts and move on.

Also be aware that the kiss of death can come from nice people. They will agree with everything you say, just to be nice. These people are easy to get by, but getting by people is not your goal. You want them to buy in, because that's the only hope you have of having a satisfied investor. Inevitably, as you get deeper into the process, you are going to run into the not-so-nice person, and when he or she starts asking all the nice people why they like your firm and doesn't get the right answers, your journey is over. If a prospect says he or she understands your firm but you can tell that he or she doesn't, the first thing you should do is verify whether you are speaking to the right person, as follows.

> *Life science fundraising executive*: "Ms. Prospect, it doesn't sound like you're the person I should be talking to."
>
> *Prospect*: "I'm not really. I'm just sitting in for Phil, who's on vacation."
>
> *Life science fundraising executive*: "Perhaps I should call Phil when he's back and set up another meeting."
>
> *Prospect*: "Yes, that would be a good idea."

Now we're getting somewhere. However, it is also possible that this is the prospect and you have to find a way to help her understand your firm even as she's saying she does. Moving the process along before a prospect understands your firm will come back to haunt you. You must make sure that everyone along the way gets it, no matter what. Don't let yourself slip or you could hurt yourself!

The Battle for Control

You should never give up an opportunity to influence an allocation. Most life science fundraising executives, however, let these opportunities slip by time after time. Here's a common scenario: a fundraising executive has a meeting with a prospect. At the end, everyone agrees to a follow-up meeting. Someone at the meeting volunteers to organize the next meeting—and the fundraising executive lets him or her.

Just like that, the process has moved out of the fundraising executive's sphere of influence.

A smart fundraising executive doesn't let this happen. He or she sees that the ball is in play and grabs it before anyone else: "Hey, it's my job to move this along. I'll call so-and-so, get a list of who should be there, schedule it, and write up an agenda." The savvy fundraising executive realizes that after people leave the meeting and get involved in their regular work, it's unlikely that setting up the next meeting will be their top priority. If the fundraising executive doesn't step up to the plate, he or she will be stuck waiting on the prospect rather than able to move forward.

You must be vigilant and not let any chance to exert your influence elude your grasp. It is of paramount importance that you take advantage of any opportunity to move the process forward. Even the simplest and seemingly most innocuous of gestures (as in the example mentioned above) can halt the allocation process. That is why you must be aware of every detail along the way.

Your Time and Your Pipeline

Use your time wisely. If you spend a lot of time working to convert your target investors to prospects and you do it well, you will succeed. To ensure your targets and prospects are always on your mind, have a list with the status of each in front of you at all times (see Figure 13.1). I recommend placing a whiteboard in your office and marking it with three columns:

- *Identified.* These are the investors with whom you have not spoken but who fit your predetermined investor profile.

- *In Play.* These are qualified investors with whom you have begun to have an ongoing dialogue by phone or email or in face-to-face meetings.

- *In Process.* These investors are conducting due diligence, asking for information, and monitoring your performance. You have received a verbal and understand the general timing of the allocation.

You must ensure that you are in charge of your own list. In some cases, life science fundraising executives choose to create a list via a customer relationship management (CRM) system or a list management application. This can very useful, and you can read more about creating this kind of cloud-based infrastructure in Chapter 8, but when it comes to the top 10 companies I want to watch, I always put them on my white board. No matter how you organize them, remember that you are going to be tracking interactions with many potential investors; as I've stated over and over, canvassing the market for investor fits is a numbers game.

After you put each investor target or prospect into one of these three categories, write down your next action or task for each. Then, any time anyone approaches your desk say, "Hey, here's my list and some ideas for

FIGURE 13.1: *A graphical representation of identifying fits and the gradual process toward receiving an allocation*

getting to the next step. What do you think?" Get everyone's opinion.

Start every day by reviewing your list and either taking action or thinking about what you can do to move each investor target or prospect along. "Moving them along" means moving them into the next stage or getting them off the list. Working through your list can take 20 minutes or it might take all day. After you do all you can, start to work on getting new targets—but only until the end of the day. The next morning, start again at the top with your hottest prospect and think about how you can move that process along on that day. Take whatever action you can, then move down to number two, and so on.

A big pitfall many life science fundraising executives fall into is beginning their day by focusing on their lukewarm prospects. This often causes them to spend their entire workday on them; by 5:00 PM they haven't spent a minute on their hot prospects. This makes no sense.

The way to fundraise effectively is to first focus on the investor targets and prospects that are furthest along in the process, every day. Taking this time daily to be thoughtful regarding your approach will make fundraising much easier. Another big mistake many fundraising executives make is that they don't stop to think. They like to take action and make things happen. Earlier I mentioned that cultivating prospects takes patience. It also requires a nimble strategy. Not only do you need to create a profile of who you need to go after and devise a game plan *before* you approach investor targets and prospects, but you also must consistently revisit your plan and anticipate the prospect's actions and your reactions *while* you're in an allocation process.

Summary

I hope this book has provided some insight regarding capital fundraising in the life science arena. Hopefully it has shed some light on the basic elements of fundraising, including aggregating a list of bona fide investor targets that are a fit for you, your team, your firm, and your product, and utilizing some inexpensive, Web-based cloud applications to help manage your target list and associated tasks. I also hope you have come away with some insight on what to expect as you undertake this process and understand that you and your team will have to stay flexible and adjust your strategy and message as you execute your outbound campaign.

If you do not have previous sales and marketing experience, launching an outbound fundraising campaign can be a daunting undertaking. Acquiring a new skill set and learning a new language is never easy, and only your internal desire can drive your capability to succeed at this endeavor. Just as important as embracing this role is coming to understand, after learning about this new universe of sales and marketing, that you may not be the ideal person to lead the charge. Either way, now you can move forward with a thorough understanding and appreciation of the entire allocation process and how an outbound fundraising campaign works.

I founded Life Science Nation to help move science forward by trying to close the funding gap that exists between new emerging technology and the investors that are eager to assist in its development. Connecting emerging life science companies with emerging life science investors is what drives my LSN colleagues and me, and I feel blessed to be successfully making this passion a reality every day. I hope this crash course in fundraising campaign management has enlightened you and serves as a useful tool as you move forward to achieve your own goals and dreams.

CHAPTER 14

Thirty-One Tips for Effective Fundraising

This portion of the book is designed to be a quick reference that combines a little bit of my philosophy interspersed with some methodology and tactics. So sit back, relax, and let me entertain you with an illustrated guide to the finer points of navigating the fundraising process.

Think of this as your cheat sheet—something to peek at before you get on a conference call or head into a face-to-face meeting. It's also a good way to stay in tune with your inner marketer. Fundraising is a simple process, yet sometimes it's hard to stay focused amid the hustle and bustle. These general rules will help, if you keep them in the front of your brain at all times. So without further ado, let's get started.

1. Have a Good Attitude

Repeat after me: it is OK to laugh at ourselves and the predicaments we find ourselves in. It is your attitude that will make you or break you every single second of every single day. Wake up with a good attitude and the world just works right. Wake up with a bad attitude and the sky is falling and the earth is moving under your feet. Keep your attitude adjusted. Be positive. Be upbeat. Be optimistic. The alternative is not for the faint of heart!

2. Get Organized Already!

Something that promotes a good outlook is being organized. We all need to keep track of tasks and contacts and make reporting our progress easier.

Unfortunately, many marketers spend inordinate amounts of time "getting organized." This often manifests itself in the form of excessive self-education or studying the latest marketing theories. Some are true in their pursuit of enlightenment; others are simply procrastinating. Either way, though, too much time on this is a waste of precious hours.

You've got targets to call and a pipeline to fill. For the love of Pete, do not let self-help turn into an act of self-mutilation!

3. Teamwork Gets You Where You Need to Go

There will be days when you feel like a one-person SWAT team and your inner Rambo is ready to take the hill. Don't go it alone. It really takes teamwork—in the beginning, in the middle, and at the end—to win an allocation. So build your team and practice with your team, for when the game is afoot, you will surely need them.

4. Be You

A frequent barrier to effective marketing is self-image. For many scientists, the stigma of selling can make it challenging to jump head-first into an outbound campaign. Will we look bad if we go outbound? Will I look desperate by aggressively marketing my asset? Is an outbound fundraiser really just a salesperson? Egad! What has become of me?

Stop that, right now. Be who you are: an entrepreneur. What's important is that your efforts are keeping your firm afloat and helping to move your asset forward. There's no shame in that. So be proud of who you are. Don't try to hide. Now that I have gotten you to accept who you are and what you do, you can fire your psychiatrist.

5. Protect Your #1 Asset—You!

You can't be successful unless you're feeling fit and on top of your game. The world you inhabit is stressful. You need to keep your mind and body in shape to deal with the stress. I am a big believer in working out three times a week. You, too, should make a point to get into a regular program. Pronto!

6. Ya Gotta Believe!

We have covered attitude, organization, teamwork, self-image, and, of course, de-stressing and staying in shape. All this gets topped off with the concept of *believing*. You must believe you can raise capital for your fund. True and earnest belief is as important as a strong work ethic. We all know folks who have the odds stacked against them, who don't seem to have a blessed chance in the world, yet they have goals so big that you wonder if they're right in the head. Then they succeed—they fly to the moon, make

their millions, win the World Series (case in point: the Red Sox in 2004)—and everyone is amazed. Is it a fluke? No, it's believing!

7. Who's Who in the Zoo

Diligence and hard work are musts. That goes without saying. You also need to be savvy and understand all the players on your team and all the players at your prospect companies. There are no two ways about this. You need to figure out who's who in the zoo.

8. Stick with Your Program

Speaking of those inside and outside your firm, make sure you spend your time with people who add to your productivity. It is easy to let folks distract you from your mission. It is easy team up with colleagues who don't have the drive and motivation that you need to have. Such associations will derail you. Shun those who do not share your goals.

9. Respect Your Admins

Now let's talk about the administrative support staff in your life. They can make you or break you. In fact, the power in most organizations lies with the admins. So treat them well and show them the respect they deserve. If you don't, you might as well take the longest walk off the shortest of piers.

10. You're the Maestro of Your Reality

It is you who must be the conductor of your orchestra. You are the person with the baton in hand, and it is up to you to get the orchestra ready for prime time. Everyone is watching you. Everyone awaits your signal. Once you start the performance, you can't miss a beat.

11. Sweat the Small Stuff

Although you may be directing the show, you also have to be aware of the details. There is a saying that the devil is in the details, and it's true. Pay attention to the details at every point in the fundraising cycle. If you do not worry about the "little things," they will get you in the end and sink your ship. Be a sleuth, be a worrier, sweat the small stuff. Securing an allocation is all about taking care of all the details.

12. Call 'Em as You See 'Em

Securing an allocation is also about doing the right thing. You are the arbitrator of what is right and what is wrong. You and you alone have to make the call. You must summon your integrity and strength and call it like you see it. So many horror stories could be avoided if someone would only blow the whistle and lay down the rules of engagement.

13. A Fit Is a Fit

Another thing to keep in mind is the all-important concept of "fit." Develop an investor profile that matches your company's needs and then go after investors who fit that profile. This saves time on both sides of the table. Do not busy yourself trying to jam square pegs into round holes. A fit is a fit. If not, move on.

14. Connect the Dots

The universe of marketing is all about collecting data points and analyzing them to gain insight and an edge. This is basic Dot Connecting 101. The one who connects the dots the quickest will find the straightest path to cash. This means gathering clues from your experiences, your colleagues, and the marketplace and then connecting the dots to see a picture of how you can be successful.

15. Dial in Your Audience

The goal of a fundraiser is to find investor targets that are a good fit. This requires creating an investor profile. Think about it. How can you go out into the investor universe if you do not know who you are looking for? Take the time and create a crisp and cogent investor profile. Once you do, you'll see how easy it is to find targets.

16. Focus on Good, Qualified Leads

One of the conundrums for most fundraisers is sticking with the investor profile that fits their company. They compile lists and buy databases of all the life science investors (there are only about 5,000 of them on the planet), but they don't vet the leads. You must divide the targets into categories and be very rigid about who is NOT a fit and who you will NOT pursue. Going after an investor who is not a fit is a waste of time for both parties.

17. Keep Your Cool

Many times you have to double your efforts to identify and produce good prospects. Having a bunch of leads on your desk or in your database that are not a fit and not qualified can get you in a fix pretty quickly. When they know they are short of good qualified leads, some fundraisers fall down the desperation rat hole. They get fearful, start to lose their cool, and forget to match targets against their investor profiles. They start emailing and calling randomly. AVOID DESPERATION.

18. Be Tactical on Your Trips

Remember, looking for prospective investors can be done in a mellow state with a preplanned strategy. Look at sections of your geographic turf as a prospect mall. Like all malls, there are probably three to five anchors (big prospects), the secondary players, and some smaller players. So if you are calling on a big pharma corporate venture arm, figure out which family offices and other small investors are nearby. There is nothing wrong with killing two birds with one stone.

19. Seek and You Shall Find

One of the keys to effective prospecting is taking the time to really vet your territory. This means leaving no stone unturned. It is hard work, but it will pay off, because the harder you work the more prospects you will turn up.

20. Take Your Scientist on the Road

After you have identified your target group of investors, you need to organize conference calls and face-to-face meetings. For these you'll need the guy from the lab. Alert the person who is actually doing the R&D to the importance of these calls and meetings and his or her participation. There's no way around this one.

21. Answer All Questions

When you get out on the road and in front of investors who have mandates for your type of asset or company, then you are beginning the process. You are presenting your opportunity and answering questions. Answering questions is a BIG part of the process. You must be the one who knows the questions investors will ask and how to prepare your team to provide the answers.

22. Find the One with the Keys

Once you find a good fit, you have to map it. One of the folks you need to identify is the gatekeeper. The gatekeeper is the one in the organization who decides who will get in and who will be kept out. The gatekeeper makes sure that everyone gets the message: "If an outsider surfaces, send them unto me."

23. No Belly Bumping

Here is a topic to ponder. Belly bumping! A big issue, particularly in the life science industry, is ego. Let's face it, there is a lot of intellectual fire-power in the biotech and medtech arena, and some folks like to think of themselves as the smartest guys in the room, the cream of the crop, the raconteur bons vivants. The issue with these people is that they tend to enjoy flaunting their intellect—sometimes at the wrong time. So when you drag your chief science officer out of the lab to make an investor presentation, show him or her this cartoon and say, "Please, please, please, no belly bumping today."

24. Find a Navigator

Upon meeting with an investor for the first time, your mission should be to try to identify the navigator and cultivate a relationship with him or her.

The navigator is the person on the other side of the table who has some skin in the game. The navigator knows the firm well and will be able to guide you through the unfamiliar territory that you have to navigate to engage in a successful dialogue. The navigator is your inside go-to person. Most entrepreneurs who win allocations have taken the time to map the players who have participated in creating the mandate, and they have uncovered the gatekeeper and the navigator.

25. Hit the Reset Button

There are many players who come in and out of the picture during the course of the allocation cycle. It is imperative that you keep tabs on all of them. As a matter of fact, any time a new player comes into the fray, it is vital that you hit the reset button, start from the top, and go back to square one. Let them know who you are and why you are here. The most important aspect of marketing is keeping everyone in context, constantly. It is a daunting task, but it makes all the difference in the world.

26. Good Things Come to Those Who Work Hard

If you can keep all of the points I've mentioned in the front of your brain, then a dialogue will start with the investor. The phone will be ringing, the emails will be coming in, there will be meetings to schedule, and you will be in what I like to call "the mix." This is truly the most fun part for a marketer.

27. Hang in There Until the Last Question Is Answered

It is precisely at this time when fundraisers need to be vigilant. This means being aware of any outstanding issues. I have a theory that when the last question is answered to the investor's satisfaction, then an allocation is just around the corner.

28. Patience Is Suffering

Just before the allocation, however, beware of the dead zone. The dead zone is that place in time when everything that has to be done is done and now you wait. Depending on the category of investors and the length of their allocation cycle, this can be inordinately torturous. But this is how it is with the allocation process in the fundraising arena. You must learn to suffer gladly! I mean, you really have no choice. If you have done your job and all is right with the world, then allocations will be forthcoming.

29. Remember to Nurture Your Investor Prospects

There is inevitably a dead zone in every fundraising cycle, but if you have been doing the right things throughout the process and taking care with

the opportunity, then all will be fine. When in the dead zone, do not panic and do not overreact. Be respectful of the investor's time. Go about your business of cultivating the next potential investor. There is no option but to keep busy.

30. Have Faith and the Cash Will Come

Eventually, the phone will ring, the email will come, or the bank account will show a wire transfer, and you will have secured an allocation!

31. Know When to Stop Marketing

At this point, it's critical to remember the golden rule: when you're done, you're done. Cease and desist with the pomp and circumstance. When you have secured an allocation from an investor, stop marketing to them. Your job is done.

SECTION FIVE

Addendum

The View Beyond Venture Capital

Dennis Ford & Barbara Nelsen

This article first appeared in Nature Biotechnology, Volume 32, 2014.

Fundraising is an integral part of almost every ayoung biotech's business strategy, yet many entrepreneurs do not have a systematic approach for identifying and prioritizing potential investors—many of whom work outside of traditional venture capital.

Are you a researcher looking to start a new venture around a discovery made in your laboratory? Perhaps you have already raised some seed money from your friends and family and are now seeking funds to sustain and expand your startup. In the past, the next step on your road to commercialization would doubtless have been to seek funding from angels and venture capital funds; today, however, the environment for financing an early-stage life science venture looks strikingly different from that familiar landscape of past decades.

Following the economic downturns of 2008 and 2011, the profiles of those investing directly in biotech startups have changed; many traditional investors have curtailed their mandates and reduced their allocations to early-stage life science companies, and new types of investment entities have emerged in their stead. Entrepreneurs also have to come to grips with the shifting regulatory environment that defines how private capital is raised, who can serve as liaisons between entrepreneurs and investors and the type of individuals who can participate in financing a startup (**Box 1**).

If you are seeking funds for a startup, you need to be aware of the range of investors and investment vehicles available, as well as the pros and cons of each route. In this article, we provide a brief primer to help you navigate your path through the new investor landscape and find the right investment partners for your company.

BOX 1 State and federal fundraising regulations in flux

The US National Institutes of Health has redefined who can qualify for Small Business Innovation Research (SBIR) loans, opening the program up to companies who have venture capital investors, which was formerly a barrier to qualification. In addition, the passing of the Jumpstart Our Business Startups (JOBS) Act has added complexity to the regulatory environment surrounding financings, with Title II of the Act allowing companies to raise capital through general solicitation of accredited investors and Title III allowing companies to crowdfund equity investments from unaccredited investors. Federal and state laws have heavily enforced regulation on exactly who can invest—only those above a certain income and net worth can be deemed an accredited investor. Currently, these two new exceptions created by the JOBS Act cannot be used together as part of the same fund-raising round, which leaves startup companies in a contradictory legal landscape.

In addition, the Financial Regulatory Authority and the Securities and Exchange Commission have clearly stipulated that any person or entity representing buyers and sellers of securities must be licensed to do so. As an aspiring entrepreneur in the life science arena, you will encounter a myriad of finders of capital, professional deal sourcers, third-party marketers, broker dealers and investment banks all aiming to connect you with capital. The important take-home message is *caveat emptor*, or buyer beware. The gray space surrounding the legal environment is in flux, and thus the viability of the entities involved in the raising of capital must be vetted and understood

---

Why and how did the funding landscape change?

The big changes in the life science investor landscape start with the venture capitalist (VC). In the past, venture capital funds were typically capitalized by large institutional investors that consisted of pensions, endowments, foundations and large family offices with $100 million to $1 billion in capital under management. Traditionally, the majority of these institutions maintained a low-risk, low-return portfolio of stocks and bonds that offered predictable and stable returns. A few decades ago, fund managers adopted a strategy of putting a small portion of the assets under management into higher-risk, higher-return vehicles, such as hedge funds, private equity funds and venture capital funds. This generally worked well until the 2008 and 2011 economic downturns.

During the downturns, it quickly became apparent that entrusting capital to third-party alternative fund managers was no longer an effective strategy, and investors began to withdraw capital. The main reason for the withdrawal (especially from VCs in the early-stage life science space) was generally meager returns across the asset class; despite the high risk and long lockup periods that investors accepted in return for a promise of premium performance, VCs were often not returning any more capital than investors would have earned by making more liquid investments in the public small caps market. Returns from venture capital funds have not outperformed the public markets since the late 1990s (ref. 1). A second reason was that returns earned by investing in VCs were offset by substantial costs; fund managers typically charged a 2% management fee on the money they received. This of course is palatable when a manager is returning great profits but is not such a strong proposition during a period of consistent losses. Yet another reason for the withdrawal, and the most troubling, was that a general lack of transparency and long lockup periods turned many funds into 'capital traps' from which investors could not withdraw and were unable to influence the decisions of the managers.

Many VCs failed to prove to institutional capital managers that they were capable of identifying and vetting winners in the life science sector despite being paid handsomely to do just that. That said, of course there remains a subset of early-stage VCs who consistently pick winners and have outperformed through these tough times, but these well-known firms are in a distinct minority. Lack of returns and steep

management fees became a bone of contention that prompted a lot of institutional investors to withdraw their capital from the fund managers and instead do their own alternative investing. Thus, VCs lost a valuable funding source (a Kaufmann Foundation report details one institution's reflections on backing away from VC investments)[2] and, as a result, institutional investors and large single- and multi-family offices often do direct alternative investment—essentially, taking a similar percentage of their funds and investing in early-stage opportunities with the same potential for high returns but in which the institution maintains control rather than ceding oversight to a VC. These investments can occupy anywhere from 2–10% of their assets under management.

This change in tactical investment technique coincides with a growing trend for passion, philanthropic and social investment as part of an investor's criteria. This is especially so in the life science sector, in which the social impact of investment dollars can be huge. New, more engaged and informed investment vehicles such as patient groups and philanthropic venture funds have entered the space formerly occupied by underperforming VCs.

Corporate pharmaceutical companies are also undergoing drastic strategic changes. Facing aging portfolios of on-the-market drugs and an impending patent cliff, big pharma must restock the pipeline with innovative assets, and many companies are turning to academic research collaborations, licensing, investment—through corporate venture capital—and mergers and acquisitions as an alternative to in-house R&D at the early stage. This cherry-picking strategy of plucking innovation emerging from academia has become a ubiquitous strategy among the top pharmaceutical firms globally. Big pharma not only offers a huge source of capital for early-stage companies but also provides access to distribution channels for the market, discovery and development expertise and many other resources.

In addition, across the space, many of the remaining active VCs, new virtual pharmaceutical firms (for example, Eli Lilly's Chorus Group, based in Indianapolis; Karolinska Development, based in Stockholm; Accelerator Corp., based in Seattle; Apple Tree Partners, based in Princeton, New Jersey; and Velocity Pharmaceutical Development, based in San Francisco) and mid-level private equity entities (for example, Hercules Technology Growth Capital, based in Palo Alto, California; Burrill & Co., based in San Francisco; Omnes Capital, based in Paris; and Auxo Management, based in Mississauga, Ontario, Canada) are executing a business model of buying assets low, developing them through early-stage clinical trials and then selling them high. These entities essentially institute a strategy of aggregating low-cost, early-stage assets around particular indications, outsourcing the clinical process and then developing or redefining channel relationships that can create outsized returns. They aim to maximize capital efficiency and create a lean portfolio of high-quality assets primed for market entry.

Focused investor mandates versus opportunistic investors

Two investment strategies dominate in today's investor environment. One is based on using traditional market analysis and creating a structured mandate to invest in a particular sector's products and/or services. Typical considerations include determining which key indication areas or phases of development will bring the greatest return on investment. This type of 'deep dive' market analysis will consider major epidemiological, macroeconomic, demographic, regulatory and reimbursement shifts. The result is a so-called investment mandate. The investor has predetermined what sector, indication and stage of development they wish to pursue and formalized the resulting research data into a specific set of criteria for investment. Remember, investing in an early-stage venture means getting in for less capital and more risk, and these two factors are all part of the bet. The goal of any life science entrepreneur is to find an investor that is a fit. Matching an investment mandate with your company's offering is one tried-and-true way to be considered for funding.

On the other end of the spectrum are opportunistic investors—ones that do not limit their investment mandates to a particular sector or indication (for example, small molecule or gene therapy, or diabetes or oncology). Rather than betting on a specific technology, disease, development phase or service, an opportunistic investor wants to play in the entire life science arena, and they believe that creating a specific mandate would limit the rest of the market outside that mandate; they prefer to pick and choose anything interesting and exciting that surfaces. This could be the latest groundbreaking medical device, a new dynamic therapeutic or a next generation diagnostic capability; all are fair game to an opportunistic investor. Oftentimes, these are 'gut' investors who are driven by a belief in the technology and/or management team, and they make judgments on a one-off basis regarding whether or not to allocate.

This dual dynamic of specific mandate versus opportunistic investment strategy permeates all the categories of life science investors, and indeed each has its upsides and downsides. Because there are experts in both strategies with capital to invest, a fundraising entrepreneur must be aware of this dynamic.

You will hear opinions from all over the life science universe about how to find investors and create a dialog with them. Life Science Nation (LSN), based in Boston and for which Dennis Ford is CEO, distributes a weekly newsletter that covers and frames current perspectives on life science investment (http:// blog.lifesciencenation.com/).

The investor landscape has changed, and the old and new categories of investors are morphing as the life science market changes and moves forward (**Fig. 1**). Let us take a fresh look at the current lineup of life science investors.

Getting started

Raising funds for a venture is a process not wholly unlike that of obtaining grants for research. Not only do you need to identify and approach the right funding bodies (and ascertain that you are eligible and understand how much money is available) but also you need to appreciate what specific areas of research are 'hot', what the application guidelines are and how to tailor your application to best appeal to evaluators and showcase your research so you have the best chance of getting an award.

Beyond turning to the people who know you best and already have cause to believe in you (friends and family), the key to fundraising success is identifying the right pool of potential investors for you (**Box 2**). Some of these are tradi-

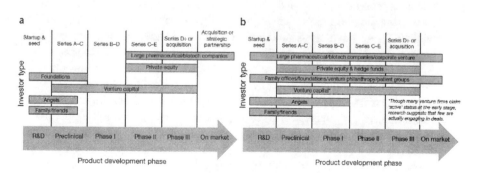

Figure 1 *The life science investor landscape. (a) The traditional landscape. (b) What the new landscape looks like.*

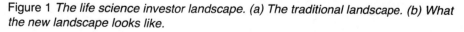

BOX 2 A glossary of investors

Angels. High–net-worth individuals usually with an interest in a particular type of product, service or industry. Many are successful entrepreneurs themselves.

Corporate venture capital. Large pharmaceutical and biotech companies' investment arms. For these strategic funds, investments are driven not only by financial returns but also by the development of relationships that could lead to future strategic collaborations and product opportunities.

Family and friends. These personal contacts typically provide capital for products that are in the earliest phase and are drawn to invest on account of a close connection to the founders of the company. As they are not professional investors and may lack familiarity with the life science industry, they may not have realistic expectations for the development of the venture. Using these personal bonds as a source of capital runs the risk of straining them.

Family offices and/or private wealth. Family offices and/or private wealth firms represent the collective estate and assets of ultra-high- net worth individuals. They have large amounts of capital, a sophisticated institutional approach toward investments and a long-term outlook, and many also have an interest in philanthropy.

Foundations, nonprofits and patient advocacy groups. Often grouped under the heading of venture philanthropy, these groups not only provide grants for basic academic research but also use venture investing principles to speed the development of drugs in their areas of interest and return capital for the fund's future work. (For an inventory of these groups, see http://train.fastercures.org/TRAINInventory/).

Federal government. In the United States, federal funds are available from the Small Business Innovation Research Program (SBIR), the Small Business Technology Transfer Program (STTR) and the US National Institutes of Health, in addition to other government departments that have an interest in some specific life science projects, such as the Department of Defense or Department of Agriculture.

Regional economic development agencies. Economic development groups provide resources to start companies locally. These can take many forms such as job growth incentive tax credits, the Strategic Cash Fund Incentive, enterprise zone tax credits, local government initiatives, state college spin-out funds and venture capital funds seeded by regional governments. Visit your local and state economic development agencies to learn the variety of resources available to you.

Super angels. Large groups of angels that increase the effectiveness of angel dollars. These investors have organized themselves into regional or national networks to increase the size of their investment pool and develop new strategies.

tional funders of early-stage ventures who will doubtless be familiar to you but whose attitudes toward investing are changing; others are new players in the space or new entities entirely.

Venture capital. Historically, venture capital has been a primary source of funding for startup and growth companies, but in recent years the life science space has witnessed a contraction of venture capital funds, with many active funds moving investments to later-stage companies. First-round funding has especially fallen off.

Data from the National Venture Capital Association in Arlington, Virginia, and media and information firm Thomson Reuters in New York show that in 2006, 294 first-round allocations were placed into life science companies, representing 23% of the total; by 2012, the corresponding figures had decreased to 149 rounds and 12.8%. In fact, 2012 saw the lowest level of first-round venture capital financings of life science companies since 1995 (ref. 3). A recent evaluation of deals by the online newsletter *Xconomy* cites only 32 venture capital firms investing in early-stage life science companies in the past few years[4]. Financial database provider PitchBook, based in Seattle, recently published a report that documents the decline in volume of VC deals while showing that the median valuation of companies receiving venture capital funding has been rising[5]— a sure indication that VCs are backing away from risky early-stage projects and are instead putting their shrunken supply of dry powder into less risky, more developed companies.

One additional wrinkle on the early stage investment landscape is that many venture capital firms, such as Atlas, Third Rock and Flagship, all based in Cambridge, Massachusetts, now create companies in house and are not typically conduits for funding external startups. They rely heavily on their own internal networks of key opinion leaders and entrepreneur insiders for these ventures. Kevin Starr, a partner at Third Rock, said recently, "Last year, we saw 982 outside plans. We invested in zero"[6].

The good news is that Third Rock and others are looking for transformative platforms and technologies to build new companies. If you are thinking of starting a company, you should consider developing relationships with these funds and their partners now. All have scientific advisory boards, and all use scientific domain experts to evaluate opportunities. Let them know who you are, your area of expertise and why you are interested in working with them.

Corporate venture capital. The corporate VC is distinct from a traditional VC on many levels. Corporate VCs are largely the product of profound shifts among large pharmaceutical and biotech companies. As mentioned previously, an aging marketable drug portfolio among the top pharmaceutical companies has led to a scramble for assets to feed dry pipelines. In the past, such pipeline gaps would be filled by the work of in-house pharmaceutical R&D, but in recent years this internal research has been cut from big pharma's budgets. Instead, companies have been finding it more cost effective to outsource the risks of early-stage research by acquiring emerging assets from third parties and by making use of virtual development services.

Entrepreneurs and scientific founders need to appreciate the distinction between corporate development and corporate venture. Corporate venture capital invests in companies developing breakthrough technologies that the firm believes have long-term disruptive potential; corporate development seeks to make tactical partnerships to fill near-term pipeline requirements by purchasing or licensing an asset. Because of this distinction, pharmaceutical companies often provide several different funding sources for emerging companies. This fundamental business change is creating more opportunities for startups to engage with the pharmaceutical giants, which offers great possibilities for a new entrepreneur.

Recently, several pharmaceutical firms have launched innovative fund concepts targeting life science entrepreneurs. For example, both the Novartis Option Fund and the Boehringer Ingelheim Venture Fund, which recently opened in Cambridge, Massachusetts, provide seed capital to highly innovative ventures, and Lilly Ventures funds external molecule development[7]. More information about pharmaceutical venture funds specifically focused on university inventions and spin-outs is provided in **Table 1**, and information on databases can be found in **Box 3**.

Table 1 Venture and hybrid funds for institutional inventions and startups

Fund name	Website
5AM Venture Management	http://5amventures.com/
Allied Minds	http://www.alliedminds.com/
Atlas Venture	http://www.atlasventure.com/
BioMotiv	http://www.biomotiv.com/
Canaan Partners	http://www.canaan.com/
Connecticut Innovations	http://www.ctinnovations.com/
Domain Associates	http://domainvc.com/
Flagship Ventures	http://www.flagshipventures.com/
Illinois Ventures	http://www.illinoisventures.com/
Kleiner Perkins Caufield & Byers	http://www.kpcb.com/
Lilly Ventures	http://www.lillyventures.com/
Novartis Option Fund	http://www.venturefund.novartis.com/
Polaris Partners	http://www.polarispartners.com/
PureTech Ventures	http://www.puretechventures.com/
T1D Innovations	http://jdrf.org/
Third Rock Ventures	http://www.thirdrockventures.com/
Sofinnova Ventures	http://www.sofinnova.com/
State venture capital funds	http://www.treasury.gov/resource-center/sb-programs/Documents/VC%20Report.pdf
SV Life Sciences	http://www.svlsa.com/
Venrock	http://www.venrock.com/

BOX 3 Databases and other resources to start your search for investors

You will need to find the database providers producing the most relevant and up-to-date information to help you in your search for investors. In choosing a source, you will want to understand how the database aggregates information. Some of these vendors collect data by amassing publicly available content such as press releases. Others follow websites that cover licensing deals or financings that have been made public, or they consolidate articles from certain publications. The databases with the most up-to-date information leverage a team of researchers to collect data through one-on-one interviews with investors. The fresher the data, the more effective and efficient you can be in fundraising. To help start your search, we provide a list of starting points for a search in **Table 5** below.

Table 5 Advisors and/or database providers that can help your search for early-stage life science investors

Database	Website
Angel Capital Association	http://www.angelcapitalassociation.org/
Angel Resource Institute	http://www.angelresourceinstitute.org/
BioCentury	http://www.biocentury.com/
Biotechgate	http://www.biotechgate.com/
FasterCures	http://www.fastercures.org/
FreeMind	http://freemindconsultants.com/
Life Science Nation	http://lifesciencenation.com/
Massinvestor	http://www.massinvestor.com/
National Venture Capital Association	http://www.nvca.org/
Thomson Reuters	http://www.recap.com/

Angels. In addition to family and friends, angels and 'super angels' typically provide capital for companies that are in the earliest phase. In 2012, angels invested a total of $1.1 billion in 783 deals (primarily in first funding), with 27% of that invested in the healthcare and life science sector[8]. National chapters, syndications with other angel funds and single-source online application platforms (for example, http://gust.com/) have made it easier for a bioentrepreneur to gain access and visibility with angel investors. Angels are now part of larger investment pools and have the ability to execute sophisticated investment strategies and provide funding at higher levels than in the past, perhaps participating in multiple rounds of financing. This makes these groups a viable form of financing your startup through an exit, depending on the capital needs and time horizon of your venture. The top ten groups in terms of activity are shown in **Table 2**. To find comprehensive information about angel investment funds, who and where they are, what they invest in and the best way to set up a meeting with them, visit the Angel Resource Institute website and the Angel Capital Association website.

Remember that you may be getting more than money when an angel fund invests in your company. An angel group can be a source of deep expertise and connections that provides more value in growing the company than the capital itself. Many life science angels are themselves successful entrepreneurs in the field and may offer you access to the resources and partnerships that supported their own success. You should put just as much effort into your business plan and investor pitch as you would when approaching a typical venture capital firm.

Government agencies. This is a very broad category ranging from funds within research institutions to local economic development initiatives to national and international entities. The level of Small Business Innovation Research (SBIR) funding is set to *grow* in the next year. If you have not already considered applying for SBIR or Small Business Technology Transfer (STTR) grants, you should do so immediately. A concise overview on how to apply for these funds was published in *Nature Biotechnology*[9].

The US National Institutes of Health has many funding options available for entrepreneurs and young companies, particularly for those conducting clinical or translational research. The total dollar value awarded for clinical research at the NIH reached more than $10 billion in 2012, and in 2013 it was larger than the total awarded to any other specific field or stage of research[10]. Eighty percent of National Institutes of Health funding opportunities are not part of the request-for-proposal process, so you will need to work directly with program directors to apply. This may seem daunting, but direct outreach to the

Table 2 Angels at work		
2012 rank by number of deals	Group	Location
1	New York Angels	New York
2	Tech Coast Angels	Southern California
3	Launchpad Venture Group	Boston
4	Central Texas Angel Network	Austin, Texas
5	Golden Seeds	New York, Boston and San Francisco
6	Sand Hill Angels	Sunnyvale, California
7	Investors' Circle	National
8	Alliance of Angels	Seattle
9	Common Angels	Boston
10	Maine Angels	Portland, Maine

2013 Halo Report, Angel Resource Institute.

agencies or to those who assist in developing nondilutive funding (for example, the FreeMind Group) is the best route[11].

Many local and regional government agency funds also exist for innovation and startups in the life science area. The most visible of these are in states, such as Massachusetts and California, that have mounted large initiatives to grow sectors of the life science industry. In Massachusetts, the $1 billion Life Sciences Initiative provides funding in multiple ways, including up to $750,000 for new life science companies to help leverage additional sources of capital. The California Institute for Regenerative Medicine (CIRM), based in San Francisco, still has $1.8 billion in unearmarked funds to invest in stem cell and regenerative medicine, and it funds companies at every stage provided they have a substantial presence in California. As with all funding sources discussed in this article, substantial research may be required to find these funds, identify their criteria for investment and determine how to apply for them. But it is well worth the time and energy; these groups are committed to the success of life science startups in their region and, in addition to funding, will offer you access to a wealth of local resources and industry expertise.

Do not be discouraged if you are not in a funding hub such as Massachusetts or California. The large number of angel funds, innovation centers and venture capital firms in these locations come with an equally high level of competition for these resources. For entrepreneurs outside of these clusters, there are many other government and economic development initiatives that can be tapped. These most often take the form of seed stage investment funds whose mandate is to facilitate startup activity from local institutions (particularly state universities) and to recruit companies to the region by offering relocation grants and access to biocluster facilities. Representative examples include Connecticut Innovations in Rocky Hill, Connecticut; the Kentucky Seed Fund in Louisville, Kentucky; the Maine Technology Institute in Brunswick, Maine; and Illinois Ventures in Chicago. Many such funds exist; in the United States, there are currently 36 state-run venture funds in 30 states[12]. Economic development groups also provide resources to start companies locally. These can many forms, including convertible debt, equity investment, infrastructure support, shared resources and tax credits, refunds and incentives. Many states also encourage innovation by providing tax credits for angel investors. To date, 27 states provide such credits (see http://www.angelcapitalassociation.org/ public-policy/existing-state-policy/). Get more information from your local or state economic development agency about options available in your area. Do not underestimate their desire to keep you local and grow the local economy. We have seen cases in which economic development groups put together new funding mechanisms to keep breakthrough technology in-state for company formation.

New sources of funding for startups

With reduced resources and less appetite for risk, VCs are moving away from high-risk, early-stage companies. Fortunately for entrepreneurs, other classes of investors are coming to the fore to take advantage of the VC retreat. These include patient advocacy groups and foundations, big biotech and pharmaceutical companies, and venture philanthropists.

Table 3 represents the results of a search we did in the Life Science Nation investor database. The goal was to ask a simple yet compelling question: How many investors and what investor category are presently interested in investing in early-stage therapeutics from preclinical discovery all the way to phase 1 trials?

There are thousands of VCs globally. Of those that Life Science Network has researched or interviewed, 572 claim that they are investing in early stage life sciences. However, stated activity does not necessarily reflect actual activity, as published deal flow metrics do not support these claims on a total basis. It is common for investors to claim that they are active to 'stay in the game', even when they are not investing.

Patient advocacy groups and foundations. Foundations, nonprofits and venture philanthropists have traditionally been more focused on funding academic research. Indeed, collectively these entities provide more than half a billion dollars in biomedical research grants annually.

Table 3 Active investors in seed/venture stage seeking discovery through phase I therapeutics

Number of investments by type of investor (number of investors)

Disease area	Angel (83)	Venture capitalist (572)	Corporate venture capitalist (50)	Endowments/ foundations (108)	Family office/private wealth (59)	Government organization (77)	Hedge fund (12)	Institutional alternative investor (54)	Big pharma/ biotech (46)	Private equity (386)	Total (1,447)
Neoplasms/cancer/ oncology	29	136	26	42	17	37	2	22	19	63	393
Infectious and parasitic	37	176	26	21	18	35	3	9	15	51	391
Nervous system	26	165	29	29	15	37	1	18	18	52	390
Cardiovascular	29	158	30	16	9	26	1	14	13	59	355
Endocrine and metabolic	27	141	29	22	11	33	3	14	16	46	342

Blood and immune	28	149	27	18	10	24	1	14	16	38	325
Digestive system	20	115	20	7	9	21	1	8	8	36	245
Eye	16	121	18	6	10	18	0	6	11	32	238
Genitourinary system	20	115	16	6	9	17	0	6	13	34	236
Mental and behavioral	18	105	20	13	6	18	2	7	10	29	228
Congenital deformity and chromosomal defects	11	92	12	9	5	14	0	5	5	21	174
External causes morbidity and mortality	15	92	13	5	5	16	0	4	4	16	170
Ear	13	91	12	5	5	13	0	2	4	15	160
Prenatal	11	86	12	3	5	13	0	3	3	15	151
Respiratory	9	56	13	10	5	13	0	12	8	25	151
Musculoskeletal and connective tissue	11	33	8	12	2	11	1	13	8	18	117
Skin and subcutaneous tissue	6	40	4	7	2	9	0	11	7	21	107
Pain and inflammation	4	7	8	1	1	3	0	0	2	8	34
Physical injury/poisoning	0	10	2	1	0	6	0	1	3	5	28
Pregnancy, childbirth and puerperium	1	8	2	2	0	0	0	1	2	0	16
Opportunistic[a]	17	219	5	9	14	6	5	14	13	218	520

[a]Investors willing to consider diseases across areas. Source: Life Science Network investor database.

Most such groups are focused on curing one specific disease, so qualifying for funding from them requires a clear connection between your innovation and their mission. Beyond the well-known groups, such as the Michael J. Fox Foundation in New York, the Juvenile Diabetes Research Foundation in New York, Susan G. Komen for the Cure in Dallas and the Leukemia and Lymphoma Society (LLS) in White Plains, New York, there are many less prominent nonprofits that also fund research, such as the Bluefield Project in San Francisco, which funds research on treatments and cures for frontotemporal dementia. Although these groups are historically best known for supporting academic research, the vast majority—90%—will now consider partnering with commercial biotech companies[13]. Partnerships can span all stages of research and development, from discovery through clinical trials. More than one-third of these entities have supported at least one clinical trial. Indeed, Todd Sherer, CEO of the Michael J. Fox Foundation has said, "We are definitely seeing the need for foundations to support companies even through a phase 2 clinical trial."

LLS provides a clear example of how the work of foundations is changing. This foundation has been in existence for 60 years, but up until 6 years ago, it funded only academic or institutional research. When funding began to migrate away from early-stage, LLS's leadership decided to change direction. According to John Walter, the foundation's CEO, "We saw that venture dollars were drying up in the blood cancer area, and there was insufficient funding going into preclinical and clinical research. So strategically, LLS made a shift to fund this gap."

In this next fiscal year, close to 30% of LLS's funding allocation will be invested in new therapies and companies that are making a difference to patients. And this strategic shift also brings success to the companies in which LLS invests. Currently, LLS is actively shepherding 15 assets through its Therapy Acceleration Pipeline program, which seeks to bring blood cancer therapies to market. These assets range from preclinical to phase 3, and LLS has successfully brought several of its Therapy Acceleration Pipeline companies toward the market with great speed. This is accomplished by collaborative resource sharing, investment and creation of the right industry connections. One notable example was when LLS provided capital to Avila Therapeutics, which was based in Cambridge, Massachusetts, to initiate clinical trials of one lead candidate; Avila was subsequently acquired by Celgene, based in Summit, New Jersey, in 2012. Another example came when LLS also committed to provide up to $7.5 million in milestone-based funding to Epizyme, based in Cambridge, Massachusetts, in 2011, which went to support a phase 1 trial for a mixed-lineage leukemia therapy.

These partnerships often focus on funding a specific project, such as a clinical trial, and may include milestone payments for development success; in the case of Onconova Therapeutics in Pennington, New Jersey, for example, LLS provided $8 million in funding to pay for a phase 3 trial. Foundations also are providing money for seed funding enterprises; for example, Beats of Laughter in Westport, Connecticut, a foundation specializing in oncology, provides tranches of $200,000 for seed investments; the Beyond Batten Disease Foundation in Austin, Texas, provides funding for ventures as well as research in academic institutions focusing on the neurological disorder; and Cures Within Reach in Skokie, Illinois, also offers funding (~$100,000) for ventures focusing on unmet needs.

Applying to a nonprofit or foundation for a basic research grant in your area of study can be an effective way to gain visibility and credibility with the organization; building these early connections can be of great use for developing and funding a startup in the future. Much like the other organizations that you are accustomed to applying to for grant funding, these organizations will put out requests for proposals for basic research and translational development projects, and they have links and program coordinators listed and accessible through their websites. Many of these groups can be accessed through FasterCures, who has The Research Acceleration and Innovation Network (TRAIN), which lists profiles for 55 organizations that provide $600 million in medical research grants annually. About half of TRAIN groups have supported at least one clinical trial, more than half incorporate advocacy efforts into their work in fighting disease and nearly 9 out of 10 partner with biotech and pharmaceutical companies. Foundations that are not able to provide you with financing may still wish to partner

with you to share other resources (for example, access to their scientific expertise) and vital research resources (for example, tissue samples or registries of patients who may be able to participate in human clinical trials).

Big biotech and pharma. In the past, large pharmaceutical and biotech companies stayed away from investments in very early-stage companies because of the amount of risk involved. Any involvement in startup companies was through their corporate venture funds. Now, however, that is changing. Several firms are looking for opportunities to fund assets in earlier stage development, and many of the larger firms have decided that early-stage direct investment may be a viable alternative to spending funds on traditional in-house R&D.

One new avenue for big biotech involvement is the creation of incubators, such as New Brunswick, New Jersey–based Johnson & Johnson's Innovation Centers in California, Boston, London and Shanghai; Boston-based Boston Scientific's center in Shanghai; and Leverkusen, Germany–based Bayer's CoLaborator in San Francisco. These centers provide early-stage researchers with space, equipment, operations, business support, industry networks and conduits to strategic partnering. By working at an innovation center, a startup can enjoy a 'big-company advantage' that is more robust than what is offered by traditional, stand-alone incubators.

Family offices. These entities are entrusted with the money of wealthy individuals and families. There are two types of family office: single-family offices (SFOs), in which a group of financial professionals manages capital for one family, and multi-family offices (MFOs), which invest on behalf of a number of client families. As maintaining a family office is expensive, SFOs tend to be the preserve of only the wealthiest; typically, SFOs are only formed by families with a net worth exceeding $100 million. These families are therefore often well known; they either own companies, such as Andersen Windows in Bayport, Minnesota; Jennie-O Turkey in Austin, Minnesota; and Hormel in Austin, Minnesota, or founded enterprises, such as Fidelity in Boston; Cargill in Minneapolis; and Carlson in Minnetonka, Minnesota. In addition to managing the vast fortunes of these families, family offices also perform other functions, such as generational planning, legal and tax services and preserving the family's legacy through philanthropic work; it is these additional functions that distinguish MFOs from other multi-client financial advisors or wealth managers.

In the past, family offices have invested in alternative assets, such as VCs and hedge funds as limited partners. But the poor returns from these funds have encouraged family offices to take more control of their own alternative investments. Some SFOs have formed family investment vehicles that invest as VC or private equity funds but which do not accept outside capital; others see direct private placements as one of a diverse range of assets in which to place the family's wealth.

Family offices have already played a role in early-stage life science investing, especially in Europe[14].

Beyond the basic distinction between SFOs and MFOs, family offices can be highly varied. Some family offices combine investment and philanthropic goals, whereas others have formed family not-for-profit foundations that are administered separately from the family's wealth-preservation activities. A family office's philanthropic work will be directed by the personal goals of the family; within the life science sector, this may mean a focus on a disease that has affected the family or a high-impact area in which the family feels it can make a real difference in the world. Like other nonprofits in the life science space, family philanthropic foundations may have historically focused on basic research but are now supporting commercial research for much the same reasons; basic research takes a long time to deliver new treatments to patients, and wealthy families want to see the social impact of their investments in a shorter time frame. As with disease foundations, receiving an academic research grant from a family foundation may serve as a gateway to future start-up funding.

Some family offices have created innovative business models to transition scientists' discoveries to commercial entities. One example is the Harrington Project in Cleveland, a $250 million US initiative to support the discovery and development of therapeutic breakthroughs by physician scientists. Created by a family office, the Harrington Project starts with a grant-funding phase open to inventors nationwide for advancing discoveries through an innovation center that supplies hands-on resources and expertise. Then inventions and platforms are moved to an accelerator, BioMotiv, to create companies.

Family offices have a reputation for elusiveness and secrecy, but LSN has discovered that this is ultimately misleading. As with other types of investor, LSN researchers call family offices and conduct interviews regarding their investment criteria. These one-on-one interviews result in written mandates approved by the family office, and companies that use LSN as a fundraising partner can vet themselves against these mandates to assess whether they are a good fit for the family office's criteria.

Like many investors, family offices often have a 'keep below the radar' mentality, as financial confidentiality and protecting proprietary strategies are of great importance to investors (perhaps more so to SFOs than to many firms because their investors are so easily identifiable and have a distinct need for privacy). However, all investment entities need some visibility to attain deal flow. A typical family office might receive a hundred blind e-mails or cold calls a week, and because many of these solicitations are poorly matched to the office, they create a lot of needless noise and wasted time. One way family offices filter their deals is to use trusted networks, such as LSN, which provide a flow of suitable opportunities that fit the firm's mandate. Being a perfect fit can be worth more

than getting a direct referral, as a referral that is a poor fit is still a waste of a family office investor's time.

More about seed funds

BioMotiv, the aforementioned institutional startup seed fund, is one of the many new funds and funding models that have arisen to address the funding gap for early-stage technologies. Some funds, such as Allied Minds in Boston, appear on the surface to be fairly traditional venture capital firms. But they have an unusual mandate—in this fund's case, commercializing early-stage, government-owned technologies to create startup companies from innovations in US universities and federal research institutions.

Another example is T1D Innovations. Recently created through a partnership between the Juvenile Diabetes Research Foundation and PureTech Ventures in Cambridge, Massachusetts, T1D is focused on finding promising, transformational ideas in the area of type 1 diabetes from research institutes and developing them from concept to company. Beyond the specific therapeutic mission, T1D's 'syndicate now' strategy is unique; the fund has attracted $30 million in funding from other nonprofits and strategic and financial investors and will use the cash to start eight to ten projects. For those projects that survive to become new spin-out companies, T1D hopes that these companies will go on to find a pharmaceutical partner to help further develop their programs, or land a series A round from traditional venture investors to get themselves off the ground.

Internal or external outbound direct canvassing

There is a risk that academics and early-stage entrepreneurs will be drawn into a Wild West of business coaches, mentors, accelerator programs and venture centers that broadcast a flood of 'expert fundraising advice' either from advisors who have not raised money themselves lately or from consultants and mentors who have not ever actually raised capital. The reality of outbound campaigns and 9–12-month fundraising roadshows is unknown to these advisors, and they may waste a new entrepreneur's time by perpetrating myths and promoting strategies from an outdated playbook. There are plenty of third-party fundraising entities that have updated, relevant experience and are indeed good. The good ones have strong connections and a current Rolodex, but their reach is often regional; the best have a global investor network.

As an early-stage entrepreneur, you have to make a fundamental judgment call as to whether you should conduct business development and investor outreach activities inhouse using your existing management team or hire one or more experienced fundraisers to do it for you (**Box 1**). If you decide it is not something your team can usefully put their time toward, the alternative is to outsource the process to a third-party fundraising partner. It is essentially a matter of matching commitment and ability and knowing what you can and cannot do. If you cannot make outbound calls and send engaging e-mails to strangers, then you need to partner with someone who can.

It costs money to raise money. Creating effective marketing materials, conducting a targeted campaign and following up on funding leads demands both a time and financial commitment, and fundraising therefore requires that you have the necessary dedication right from the start.

To raise money effectively you must think strategically. The place to start is to think about the major expenses in a money-raising campaign (**Table 4**).

Devising a strategy

Given the challenges and opportunities that this article has outlined, how should bioentrepreneurs prioritize the options potentially available for funding their new enterprises? A closer look at just a few companies who raised money in the past year shows a mix of traditional and new investors participating in a single deal (**Fig. 2**). A review of deals this past year in California and Massachusetts, the two states with the greatest amount of investment in life science, demonstrates the broad variety of these funding alternatives in addition to traditional venture capital. You should thus consider them all.

Initially, the stage of development of your enterprise is a key filter in helping to identify the types of investors that would likely be a fit. Having identified investors compatible with your stage of company development, you should then target those whose market focus and key investment criteria fit with your firm's goals and profile. Are you addressing an unmet need for a particular patient population? Does your innovation solve a problem that is relevant to the military or veterans? The answers

Table 4 Budgeting for an outbound fundraising campaign

	Required commitment	
	Time required	Estimated cost
Developing marketing materials and content		
Executive summary, two pages (professionally advised)	30–40 h	$1,000–$5,000
Pitchbook Powerpoint presentation, 10–12 pages (professionally advised)	80–100 h	$5,000–$10,000
Website (professionally built)	200–250 h	$6,000–$15,000
Investor database		
Quality investor database[a]	–	$7,000–$10,000
List and task management application (for example, http://salesforce.com/)	–	$50–$250
E-mail delivery, tracking and reporting application (for example, iContact)	–	$100–$600
Content-developing application (for example, Wordpress)	–	Typically free
Ongoing e-mail canvassing	40 h	Salary dependent
Ongoing phone canvassing	150 h	Salary dependent
Roadshow (9–12 months)		
Travel, food and hotels (regional campaign)	–	$40,000–$50,000
Travel, food and hotels (global campaign)	–	$60,000–$80,000
TOTAL COST	–	**$60,000–$120,000 (plus salary)**

[a]A quality investor database should provide about 5,000 global investors across 10 categories, allowing you to filter down to a target list of 300–500 investors that are a fit for your offering.

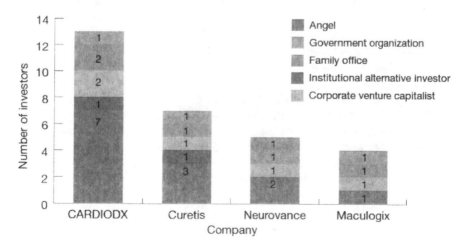

Figure 2 *Examples of investor diversity in fundraising for early-stage life science companies. Data from deals closed in the last 12 months.*

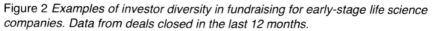

to questions like these will help you identify which of the various sources of capital described above—angel funds, foundations, nonprofits or corporate venture funds—are most likely to provide funding to you. Almost all investors have a particular focus, and identifying those that match your company will improve your fundraising chances.

Lastly, do not forget geography. Are any investors a walk, car ride or short plane trip away? This may seem an obvious approach from a logistics perspective, but there are multiple reasons to look locally. Investors need to be courted over long periods of time. Proximity makes this easier, particularly when you are engaging with smaller investment groups that have more limited footprints; most angel networks invest only in a particular locality.

It is worth considering not only your present capital needs but also your company's projected future needs. If you are developing a drug or a medical device, your company will need as much as tens of millions of dollars of external funding from several capital raises spread across a span of years before attaining a revenue stream. It is never too soon to think about what your company will need further down the line. Establishing a dialog with later-stage investors early and visiting often streamlines the financing of the organization over time, reducing the amount of effort and resources required for further rounds over the organizational life cycle.

Attempting to identify the appropriate investors to contact now and in the future can be a challenging endeavor, but there are many database services that provide information on the variety of investors available (**Box 3** and **Table 5**). These services can aid you in developing an outreach strategy tailored to your profile, position and objectives.

Conclusions

The fundraising landscape for early-stage life science companies has changed dramatically over the past several years. Venture capitalists may not always be the first, or even the most attractive, category of investor for your company. Entrepreneurs and young companies need to look toward new, emerging categories of investors to provide the funding that was historically provided by venture capital. Corporate venture funds, angels and angel networks, government agencies, foundations, patient advocacy nonprofits, family offices and hybrid funds are all actively investing in this sector.

This pace of change in the investment landscape now requires, more than ever, that entrepreneurs be nimble, informed and flexible. Creating a target list of investors that includes the newly emerging sources of capital, and focusing on those with a clear fit and strong interest in the company's stage and business, will increase the probability of fundraising success.

ACKNOWLEDGEMENTS

The authors are grateful to Maximilian Klietmann, Danielle Silva and Lucy Parkinson of Life Science Nation for research on this article. The authors would also like to thank the following individuals for their time and discussions: Vincent Miles, partner at Abingworth Life Science; Susanna Ling, associate director at the Milken Institute; John Walter, CEO at the Leukemia and Lymphoma Society; Melinda Richter, CEO at Prescience International and head of operations at Janssen Labs; Todd Sherer, CEO at the Michael J. Fox Foundation; and Ram May-Ron, managing partner at FreeMind Group.

COMPETING FINANCIAL INTERESTS

The authors declare no competing financial interests.

1. Mulcahy, D., Weeks, B. & Bradley, H.S. We have met the enemy… and he is us. *Ewing Marion Kauffman Foundation*, http://www.kauffman.org/~/media/kauffman_org/research%20reports%20and%20 covers/2012/05/we%20have%20met%20the%20enemy%20and%20 he%20is%20us(1).pdf (2012).

2. Ewing Marion Kauffman Foundation. Institutional limited partners must accept blame for poor long term returns from venture capital, says new Kauffman report. *Ewing Marion Kauffman Foundation*, http://www.kauffman.org/newsroom/2012/07/institutional-limitedpartners- must-accept-blame-for-poor-longterm-returnsfrom-venture-capital-says-new-kauffman-report (2012).

3. P ricewaterhouseCoopers. Life sciences venture capital funding drops 14% during 2012, according to the MoneyTree report. *PricewaterhouseCoopers*, http://www.pwc.com/us/en/press-releases/2013/2q-life-sciencesmoneytree. jhtml (2013).

4. Timmerman, L. Who's still active among the early-stage biotech VCs? *Xconomy*, http://www.xconomy.com/national/2012/07/02/whos-still-active-among-the-earlystage- biotech-vcs (2012).

5. P itchBook. 4Q 2013 Venture Capital Valuations & Trends Report. *PitchBook*, http://pitchbook.com/4Q2013_VC_Valuations_and_Trends_Report.html (2013).

6. L edford, H. Biotechnology: the start-up engine. *Nature* 501, 476–478 (2013).

7. von Krogh, G., Battistini, B., Pachidou, F. & Baschera, P. The changing face of corporate venturing in biotechnology. *Nat. Biotechnol.* 30, 911–915 (2012).

8. Angel Resource Institute & Silicon Valley Bank. 2012 Halo report: angel group update year in review. *Angel Resource Institute*, http://www.angelresourceinstitute. org/research/halo-report.aspx#2012HaloReport (2013).

9. Beylin, D., Chrisman, C.J. & Weingarten, M. Granting you success. *Nat. Biotechnol.* 29, 567–570 (2011).

10. US National Institutes of Health. Estimates of funding for various research, condition, and disease cate-

gories. *U.S. National Institutes of Health*, http://report.nih.gov/ categorical_spending.aspx (2013).

11. L aursen, L. Grant applications: find me the money. *Nature* 486, 559–561 (2012).

12. Cromwell Schmisseur LLC. Information and observations on state venture capital programs. U.S. Department of the Treasury, http://www.treasury.gov/ resource-center/ sb-programs/ Documents/VC%20Report.pdf (2013).

13. FasterCures. Honest brokers for cures: how venture philanthropy groups are changing biomedical research. *FasterCures*, http://www.fastercures.org/ assets/Uploads/ PDF/HonestBrokers.pdf (2013).

14. Senior, M. Family offices bolster early-stage financing. *Nat. Biotechnol.* 31, 473–475 (2013).

Adapted from Ford, D. Outsourcing your fundraising efforts: the conundrum for life science CEOs. Life Science Nation, http://blog.lifesciencenation.com/2013/02/20/outsourcing-your-fundraisingefforts-the-conundrum-for-life-science-ceos/ (2013).

Dennis Ford is founder and CEO of Life Science Nation, Boston, Massachusetts, USA. Barbara Nelsen is founder of Nelsen Biomedical, St. Paul, Minnesota, USA. e-mail: dford@lifesciencenation.com or barbara@nelsenbiomedical.com.

Reinventing Investment: The Funding Landscape of Life Science Shifts for Good

Nicole Fisher

This article first appeared on Forbes.com, March 31, 2014.

The legal landscape and requirements for a life sciences company to fundraise in the US are a nightmare, to put it gently. Guidelines changed recently with the Jumpstart Our Business Startups (JOBS) Act, and the sheer number of investment strategies for a life science startup executive to understand and pursue are staggering. Add in outdated tactics and dried up bank accounts of traditional venture capitalists (VCs), and many in the life sciences field are left jaded and skeptical about fundraising completely. Or, as Life Science Nation (LSN) Founder Dennis Ford puts it, "When I started my company, I spent 18 months traveling around the world going to tons of investor conferences, but real investors were nowhere to be found. The VCs in this space just couldn't get any returns and no longer have the money we need."

Using that premise, he set out on a mission to reinvent the way investors and entrepreneurs share information, negotiate, and now, how the markets themselves work. The premise is based on fit. Changing the preexisting shotgun approach for raising capital to a more efficient model. He has created a match.com like environment for life science investors and entrepreneurs based on targeting investors that have declared an interest in a particular sector or subsector.

According to those in the field, the future of life science investment is not the phase two and three ventures of the past. Translational and early-stage funding are the places where real value is found, and where the US investment world is headed whether investors are ready or not.

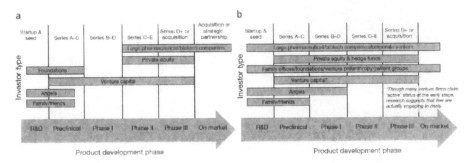

The old investor landscape (a) has shifted to a new landscape (b)

Connecting Products, Services And Capital

At LSN's most recent Redefining Early Stage Investments Conference (RESI), as many as 10 different categories of life science investors were showcased and their respective early stage investment strategies were presented and debated. Mr. Ford asserts, "Each of the categories of early stage life science investor has its own personality. Family offices, virtual Pharma's, and patient groups all have their own reason for investing, and the fundraising scientist/CEO should understand the nuances of each investor type. The RESI conference is unique because the investor panels essentially explain to the entrepreneurs how be efficient and effective in targeting the right capital."

The goal of the conference setting was not only to give life science companies a space to connect and create dialogue with potential investors, but also educate everyone in the ecosys-tem by introducing new players and strategies. The workshops and panels at RESI ranged from How to Value Your Startup to Commercialization of Academic Technology to investor debates focused on rare diseases and how orphan indications can influence investment decisions.

There is a real need for a RESI like conference, that to date has gone greatly unmet according to Susanna Ling, Director of Business and Program Development at EBD Group. "While the financial markets have improved in the biopharmaceutical sector in the past year, there is still a strong need for funding of early-stage companies and research. It is good to see quality investment opportunities matched by a diversity of investors with the flexibility to participate in new types of financial models" she says.

A new feature of the RESI conference was the RESI Challenge where 32 selected companies were given space on the exhibit hall floor to pitch their companies to investors who voted with "RESI money". Mr. Ford was delighted to announce that three female CEO's took first, second and third place.

New Roles In Investing

Ms. Ling further contends that, "The growing role of venture philanthropists, family offices, and public/private partnerships is helping to bridge the funding gap of innovative research that can go onto attract more traditional capital at a later stage of development."

While a few investment approaches presented at RESI were traditional strategies wrapped in new verbiage, most were disruptive to conventional science investment. For example, Greg Simon, CEO of Poliwogg who attended his second RESI Conference, says that, "each year a greater percentage of attendees get that this is the end of the old investment strategies and the beginning of the new. There is a lot more money available for the 97% that VCs don't look at instead of the 3% that VCs normally look at."

The premise of their work at Poliwogg, is to create platforms and metrics to let people invest in emerging companies in several ways by making the cost of entry go down.

A Fresh Take On The Old

Previously pulling together financing from the ever-expanding types of capital available was making an already complex and time-consuming fundraising process more so. Mr. Ford's com-

pany LSN also curates an early stage life science investor database. His firm covers these new investor categories through one-on-one interviews with his research team, then publishing investor profiles that are easily searched by fundraising clients. The investors are eager to participate because by declaring their interest to the LSN researcher he can get entrepreneurs that meet investment criteria.

"Non-traditional and more flexible investing models that support translational and early-stage funding are just emerging, but the JOBS Act and the power of the internet to create wide distribution will bring new investors and make these models thrive," said Sean Schantzen, whose company, Healthfundr, is building an online platform to enable these models.

Like the RESI Conference itself, "Simply pulling together everyone interested in early-stage life science investing will create enormous value for investors and startups. The internet is an enormously powerful tool to amplify relationships and participation in early-stage life science investing," said Mr. Schantzen.

More traditional lead investors such as Hub Angels Investment Group usually invests about $250K with very active involvement. However, to take financial risk out, they prefer, like everyone else, to finance alongside other angel groups.

Although, as one RESI participant joked, "When you get a conventional angel investor, it's like having a plural marriage," with lots of stakeholders making decisions.

Old Models Give Way

The shift toward new approaches for investing can also be seen spanning across new areas of the life science ecosystem, including Contract Research Organizations (CROs) and nonprofit organizations.

It is these kinds of differences in the early-stage landscape that the LSN team hope to educate life science executives on. With more knowledge of the changing scene, and targeted capital raising efforts, the entire space could become more efficient.

According to Dr. Nicole Pardo, CEO of Remind Technologies, a smartphone medication dispenser, it is working. She says her startup, "Came to RESI to explore funding opportunities for our company. We are raising our seed round and we found the conference to be a perfect mix between life science focused investors and larger companies to potentially partner with."

This new space is shifting quickly says Mr. Ford. "The news in life science is that the firmament is shifting, new investor types are filling the void vacated by the VCs, new compelling advances in technology are surfacing at an unprecedented rate, and we are entering a golden age."

Nicole Fisher is the Founder and Principal at HHR Strategies, a health care and human rights focused advising firm. Additionally, she is a Senior Policy Advisor and health policy expert on health economic analyses mainly focusing on Medicare, Medicaid, and health reform, specifically as they impact women and children. Nicole runs a Health Innovation and Policy page at Forbes.com.

About the Company

Life Science Nation (LSN) is a premier provider of investor data and market intelligence in the life science arena.

LSN operates the leading private investor database for fundraising in early stage biotech and medtech. The database is composed of easily searchable, self-declared criteria from over 5,000 active global investors. The data is curated by a research team that maintains an active dialogue with these investors on a quarterly basis to ensure current and fresh data. The platform includes profiles from family offices, angels, big pharma, corporate venture capital, private equity funds, hedge funds, foundations, venture capital funds, and other institutional-quality investors.

LSN also operates a platform of over 35,000 life science companies from around the world, with a particular focus on small and emerging companies. This data is sourced from exclusive partnerships with more than 40 of the world's largest regional bioclusters and is predominantly self-declared information. This platform provides actionable data to asset scouts, deal-sourcing professionals, and business development executives.

LSN is the producer of the Redefining Early Stage Investments Conference (www.resiconference.com), a global early stage partnering conference focused on educating early stage entrepreneurs on recent shifts in early stage fundraising. The event's purpose is to connect global life science investors with emerging technology from around the world.

LSN publishes a weekly newsletter that focuses on early stage life science investment and has a readership of over 15,000. In addition, the company sponsors a series of educational boot camps aimed at helping entrepreneurs develop branding and messaging around their technologies and learn about outbound fundraising strategies and tactics.

CPSIA information can be obtained at www.ICGtesting.com
Printed in the USA
LVOW07s1204311215

468560LV00004B/8/P